New Challenges to International Law

Nijhoff Law Specials

VOLUME 96

The titles published in this series are listed at *brill.com/nlsp*

New Challenges to International Law

A View from The Hague

Edited by

Steven van Hoogstraten

BRILL
NIJHOFF

LEIDEN | BOSTON

The production of this book has benefited from a grant by the M.A.O.C. Gravin van Bylandt Foundation in the Hague.

Cover illustration: 'Symmetry Drawing E76', Copyright The MC Escher Company BV, The Netherlands.

The Library of Congress Cataloging-in-Publication Data is available online at http://catalog.loc.gov

Typeface for the Latin, Greek, and Cyrillic scripts: "Brill". See and download: brill.com/brill-typeface.

ISSN 0924-4549
ISBN 978-90-04-38428-6 (paperback)
ISBN 978-90-04-38429-3 (e-book)

This book is printed on acid-free paper and produced in a sustainable manner.

Table of Contents
Table des matières

Introduction

Steven van Hoogstraten *

This book is a compilation of reflections on some widely divergent themes in public international law and in international criminal law. From the constitutional role of the International Court of Justice (ICJ) within the UN system to the innovation of international criminal law. From the jurisdictional complexities of the ICJ to the universal protection of human rights. The history and legacy of the International Criminal Tribunal for the former Yugoslavia (ICTY). The widely known *Yukos* arbitral award by the PCA. What these themes have in common are basically two matters. The first is that they try to identify more the underlying thoughts and considerations – what I would call the legal political considerations – than the detailed description of a subject. General impression and a helicopter view take precedence over minute description. And the second is that most of these contributions have been produced in The Hague, the international city of Peace and Justice. More in particular these reflections are in some way related to in the Peace Palace, home to the ICJ and the PCA. The Peace Palace was the result of The Hague peace treaties of 1899 and 1907 and it opened its doors in 1913 after steel magnate Andrew Carnegie donated a grand sum of money. This iconic Peace Palace has contributed so much to the image of The Hague, city of the government of the Netherlands and city of diplomats, international organizations and courts. It is for that reason that this book has the intention of giving "a view from The Hague". In so doing it shows that The Hague houses not simply a number of international institutions but that there is also a lively debate amongst academics and practitioners about the application and the

* Former General Director of the Carnegie Foundation, and Treasurer of The Hague Academy of International Law.

further development of international law in the broadest sense. By the way, the book does not go into the area of international private law, which would justify a book or two all by itself.

The Secretary-General (SG) of the United Nations has contributed much to this notion of The Hague as an international city of Peace and Justice. During the celebration of the Centenary of the Peace Palace (28 August 2013) SG Ban Ki-moon said – I was sitting on the first row opposite from where he spoke – that The Hague has effectively become "the legal capital of the world, the epicentre of justice and accountability". Being a citizen of The Hague, I was proud of that expression as it brought the notions of justice and accountability together in one phrase. Basically the work of the International Court of Justice, of the Permanent Court of Arbitration, of the International Criminal Tribunal for the former Yugoslavia, and of the International Criminal Court were combined in one thought, in one formula. As far as I am concerned, his expression should be carved in stone, and serve as the crown on the work for international justice in The Hague for over a 100 years. And it should serve as its ambition for the next century.

When the successor of Ban Ki-moon as the SG of the UN, Antonio Guterres, was in The Hague for the first time in December 2017 to be part of the conclusion of the work of the International Tribunal for the former Yugoslavia he said in his official speech, *inter alia*, "The creation of the ICTY in 1993 was a ground breaking moment. It had been close to half a century since the Nuremberg and Tokyo War Crimes Trials . . . By voting unanimously for the creation of the first ever criminal tribunal within the United Nations, the Security Council noted that it was 'convinced' that it would contribute to the restoration and maintenance of peace, thereby highlighting the close links between international criminal justice and the Organization's core mission. I would sincerely like that this feeling would remain today", said SG Guterres. The

Secretary-General must have been referring in this last part to the terrible drama of the war in Syria, where the Security Council – due to internal dissent – does not seem capable of finding an approach which even comes close to the establishment of a criminal tribunal. The best that has been done by the Security Council is the creation of an international, independent and impartial mechanism (IIIM) to assist in the investigation and prosecution of those responsible for the most serious crimes under international law committed in the Syrian Arab Republic since March 2011[1]. Incidentally, fact-finding is a very serious business. A so-called iconic picture in the press of two dead children packed in UNHCR bags and widely disseminated in the media, was found to be manipulated and specially prepared.

The foundation of this book was a seminar in the Peace Palace, on 27 January 2016 under the title "The Peace Palace, International Centre for the Peaceful Settlement of Disputes". This seminar was a marker for my departure from the Peace Palace, or better of my role of General Director of the Carnegie Foundation and Treasurer of The Hague Academy of International Law. I had been there for 13 years, from 2002. The seminar was meant to highlight some important issues related to the adjudication of justice: is it still necessary to agree on the jurisdiction of the ICJ before a case can be heard, where does the concept of arbitration go, what can be said about the constitutional role of the ICJ within the UN system? Is there a role for NGOs in legal disputes between states, should there be more emphasis on mediation in The Hague as a distinct instrument for the settlement of disputes, and so on.

This book brings together what was said on that occasion on most of the themes mentioned, even if not all the contributions could be retrieved. Fortunately some highly qualified persons

1. UN General Assembly resolution of 19 December 2016, A/RES/71/248.

offered to add to the weight of this book (in the double sense of the word) by submitting well-elaborated views on different chapters of the development of international law. That is what has led to this rather kaleidoscopic bundle. Kaleidoscopic because you will see many things and many colours in this book, and I am sure it will look a bit different every time you take another contribution as a starting point. Fortunately and following my express wish and hope, the authors have each developed a particular view. Therefore, taken together it produces a view from The Hague.

It is certain that we live in times of changes. Some will even argue that the law has to be rewritten as a result of the new technologies which have already had such an impact on our lives. The city of The Hague clearly wishes to keep pace with cyber issues, not only for reasons of staying on top of the knowledge infrastructure and being able to offer advice, but also to facilitate the resolution of disputes in the digital world. I have heard calls for a digital Peace Palace, if that were at all possible.

Changes in today's world do not only apply to new technologies, important as these may be. The composition of the world changes all the time in terms of the number of states. When the UN was founded in 1945 in San Francisco, there were only 50 states which put their name to the UN Charter, and the number is now at 193 (2018). The wave of decolonization and the general awareness of the right to self-determination have led to numerous new states, and the last chapter in this field has not been written. Take the dismemberment of Yugoslavia into several new states, such as Slovenia, Croatia, Serbia, Macedonia, and Bosnia Herzegovina. Take the particular case of the state of Kosovo, which declared independence in 2008. It has not yet been fully recognized by the world community – so far this recognition has been expressed by no more than 113 states – but it does have a special court with international judges in The Hague to deal with war crimes under the law of Kosovo. More precisely:

the Kosovo Tribunal has to deal with certain crimes against humanity, war crimes and crimes under Kosovo law between 1998 and 2000. The declaration of independence of this same Kosovo was considered by the ICJ upon request by the General Assembly (Advisory Opinion of 22 July 2010). The ICJ found in a its Opinion that the "declaration of independence did not violate international law".

South Sudan is another new state, the frontier of which to the North was judged by an arbitral tribunal created by the PCA. Catalonia was close to becoming a new state, until the Spanish Government imposed its national authority with legal force. Separation of Catalonia now seems a distant dream. Tibet is known to be in a constant struggle for self rule within China, or outside China. It was no surprise to hear the representatives of China and of Spain plead against the validation of the independence of Kosovo, during the hearings which preceded the Advice of the ICJ that I referred to. The Visitor Centre of the Peace Palace shows the original PCA chair with the impressive embroidery of the coat of arms of Austria-Hungary, a state we can hardly remember and yet so important in world history. Change is always and everywhere.

The International Court of Justice, often dubbed the World Court, is a formidable and highly respected institution. Its existence is of course defined by the Charter of the UN, supplemented by the Statute of the ICJ. It has always struck me that the informal rules about the composition of the Court and the procedures for the selection of new judges lead to a situation where the five Permanent Members of the Security Council would always have a national on the Bench. This fact is an informal situation and it is not laid down in any rule of the UN. It just happens to be so that the double key for choosing new judges (a majority is required in both the General Assembly and in the Security Council; Article 4 (1) of the Statute) leads to the presence of judges from Russia, France, the

United States, China and the United Kingdom in the ICJ. Exceptionally, the UN decided to break with this tradition in 2017 when in the final round of the elections both organs elected a judge from India and not a judge from the UK. This presence of the Permanent Five does produce an interesting question. Is it correct that the ICJ should be composed of judges from countries who did not make a declaration of acceptance of jurisdiction mentioned in Article 36 (2)? Basically we speak about the major powers in the world such as the countries just mentioned but others are concerned as well: the number of positive declarations is at only 72 out of 193 states. Should those countries nonetheless be allowed to bring a judge to the Court? I know some experts who would seriously question this, and who would state that it is better for world justice that the bench of the highest judicial organ of the United Nations be occupied by judges from countries that have accepted the jurisdiction of the ICJ as a matter of principle. I have always belonged to the opposite group who understands and defends the present composition of the ICJ. For me the main reason is the universality of the court, as it was intended by the Charter: all members of the UN are *ipso facto* parties to the Statute of the ICJ (Article 93 (1) of the Charter). In its universality the International Court of Justice is a mixture or blend of all legal systems and legal cultures in the world. It makes a difference for me – in terms of weight of a decision by the Court – to know that the legal cultures of all important parts in the world have contributed to the ultimate decision. I think that many governments respect the ICJ for the breadth of its legal image and the quality of its judgments. Decisions of such a court stand the best chance of being accepted worldwide, not only as a matter of law but also in terms of respect and standing. In short, the composition of the ICJ as it is enhances the global authority of the Court, and leaves any discussion about its impartiality and quality without arguments to lean on.

As a final remark in this Introduction, I express my profound recognition to all authors of the contributions and I thank Simone Cartier of The Hague Academy of International Law for her professionalism and dedication in the preparation and editing of this book. I was fortunate to be allowed by the M. C. Escher Foundation to use one of Escher's inimitable early works for the cover of the book.

Compulsory Jurisdiction of the Court under the Optional Clause

Abdulqawi Ahmed Yusuf*

I am very pleased to participate in this event organized in honour of Steven van Hoogstraten. I met Mr. van Hoogstraten, for the first time, in Addis Ababa, on African soil. He was there as the Treasurer of The Hague Academy of International Law, which was holding its external course for Africa and I was invited to deliver a couple of lectures there. After my election to the ICJ in 2009, I met him again here in The Hague, but this time in his capacity as Director-General of the Carnegie Foundation. As the representative of the ICJ here today, I am happy to acknowledge the crucial support he had always provided to the work of our institution and the great care he always took to ensure that we could perform our functions in a serene and agreeable environment at the Peace Palace.

My presentation will focus on the acceptance of the jurisdiction of the ICJ as compulsory under Article 36 (2) of the Statute of the Court, otherwise known as the "Optional Clause". Under this provision, a state can submit a declaration to the Secretary-General of the UN accepting the jurisdiction of the Court without requiring an agreement through which consent to the jurisdiction of the Court is given. This, as you all know, is not the sole means by which the Court can have jurisdiction over a dispute; however, it is often regarded as a litmus test for the confidence that is placed in the Court by states – a question that I will return to later in my speech.

Let me provide you with some figures that will illustrate the use of the Optional Clause. Of the 193 members of the UN, which are automatically parties to the Statute of the Court,

---

* Judge at the International Court of Justice. Elected to the ICJ in 2009, and re-elected in 2018. Elected President of the ICJ in 2018.

72 have submitted Optional Clause declarations recognizing the compulsory jurisdiction of the Court. Many have appended reservations limiting their acceptance of jurisdiction, but I do not think that anyone can deny the importance of almost 40% of states in the world recognizing one jurisdiction as the forum in which to settle their disputes. Perhaps a more enlightening statistic is the use of Optional Clause declarations as the basis for jurisdiction in cases before the Court. Of the 135 contentious cases filed at the Court, 23 establish jurisdiction on the basis of Optional Clause declarations, whereas more than double – 52 – found jurisdiction on compromissory clauses in treaties. 30 other cases found jurisdiction on both Optional Clause declarations and compromissory clauses. Although slightly less pronounced, if one looks at applications made to the Court in the past ten years, the picture is the same: of 27 new contentious cases filed, jurisdiction in 11 cases was founded on compromissory clauses whereas only eight applications relied on Optional Clause declarations.

So, contrary to conventional wisdom, Optional Clause declarations are not the be-all-and-end-all of jurisdiction; instead compromissory clauses play a significantly more important role in establishing the jurisdiction of the Court. The two common responses to this data is that the Court should either promote submission of Optional Clause declarations, increasing its use as a basis for jurisdiction, or – as the organizers of this seminar have provocatively suggested to me – that Optional Clause declarations should be confined to the annals of history as an outdated relic of the Alabama-era inter-state arbitration. Let me take these points in turn.

First, I do think that it is important to emphasize the benefits – both legal and political – of accepting the compulsory jurisdiction of the Court to states. Not only does it provide those states with a clear forum in which they can settle their international disputes, but also it demonstrates to the international community that state's commitment to the ideal of international peace and justice. When I meet representatives of states, I always emphasize the benefits of making an Optional Clause declaration. Of course, they do not have to accept the jurisdiction of the Court lock, stock and barrel or in its widest sense in each and every instance; that is both the strength and – some may say – the weakness of the system. But the ability to exclude some matters from the jurisdiction of the Court means that states are more willing to submit to the compulsory jurisdiction of the Court for other matters, and this flexibility is, in my view, absolutely crucial.

I am, however, of the view that declarations made under the Optional Clause should not be the sole focus of the Court's energy in relation to promotion of its jurisdiction. Just as important is the promotion of compromissory clauses recognizing the Court's jurisdiction in bilateral or multilateral treaties and I think that is something that the Court might need to consider in the coming years.

Turning to the second point, the organizers of this conference suggested in their "brief for the meeting" that "pre-acceptance" of jurisdiction was appropriate for inter-state arbitration, but not for the principal judicial organ of the UN. In this context, they contrasted the position of the ICJ to that of the dispute settlement mechanism of the UN Convention on the Law of the Sea and that of the World Trade Organization. They are quite right to recognize that both these treaties provide for the compulsory settlement of disputes falling within their subject-matter without requiring States to submit something like an Optional Clause declaration or to conclude a special agreement. However, this fact does not lead to the conclusion that the International Court is in some way "falling behind" more recently-conceived dispute settlement systems, nor does it support the claim that the methods of founding jurisdiction of the Court are antiquated. The dispute settlement mechanisms under both the UNCLOS and WTO Agreements operate because – and only because – states have signed and ratified those treaties, which establish a special regime. It is the consent to be bound by the provisions of the treaties – including the dispute settlement provisions – that enables the dispute settlement procedures of those special regimes to function without requiring formal consent on a case-by-case basis.

The basis of jurisdiction of the International Court, the dispute settlement institutions of UNCLOS, and the WTO panels and Appellate Body is in essence the same – the consent of states is required for a court or tribunal to adjudicate on their actions. The only difference between these institutions is the way in which states manifest this consent. The Optional Clause simply provides a means by which states can give *general* consent to adjudication, just as acceding to the UNCLOS or WTO Agreement manifests the *specific* consent of the state to adjudication through those regimes' respective dispute settlement mechanisms.

Finally, Mr. Chairman, a few more words on the Optional Clause and the widespread perception that it constitutes some sort of litmus test for confidence in the Court. States do not submit Optional Clause declarations, according to this view, because they do not have faith in the ability of the Court to effectively or efficiently adjudicate inter-state disputes, or because they prefer to take their cases to other dispute settlement forums. The conclusion normally drawn is that the Court no longer holds its traditional place at the apex of international dispute settlement, but rather is – like the myriad other courts and tribunals – just another piece in an increasingly complex mosaic of dispute settlement bodies. The lack of growth in the numbers of Optional Clause declarations is seen as emblematic of the decline of the Court.

For me, this is quite simply wrong. As I explained earlier in this presentation, the fact that some states have not submitted Optional Clause declarations says nothing about the general confidence placed in the Court. In my view, the total number of applications provides a much better picture of how states view the Court, and on that count the Court is in excellent health - almost half the total number of applications to the Court in its 70-year existence have been made in the past two decades.

Nor has the Court, in my view, fallen from its position at the apex of the international judiciary. Not only is the Court significantly busier than it was in the first 50 years of its existence, but its case law plays an important role in the reasoning of other international courts and tribunals. The WTO Appellate Body, the International Criminal Tribunals and the International Criminal Court, the International Tribunal for the Law of the Sea, as well as countless international investment tribunals, have all relied on the case law of the Court in their judgments.

Moreover, all claims regarding the place of the Court must be viewed in context. The Court was, and is, the only standing Court of general jurisdiction on the international level. Before the advent of the Permanent Court of International Justice, the idea of a standing international judiciary was a mere pipedream. The Optional Clause was then – as it is now – simply another means through which states can avail themselves of the service offered by this unique institution.

When I was reviewing Mr. van Hoogstraten's impressive CV, one thing particularly stood out – his love of cricket, demonstrated notably by his chairmanship of the national cricket board for over a decade. At first glance, cricket and the international dispute settlement mechanisms have little in common (except, one might say, the similarly-lengthy procedures). But on further reflection, the two spheres have some striking similarities – in the words of one author, cricket and the law are "simply different arenas in which struggles over meanings, interpretations, applications of rules by adjudicators . . . engage us politically, ideologically and socially". It comes as no surprise, then, that Mr. van Hoogstraten has been an active participant in both arenas throughout his career. I hope that his retirement affords him the time to appreciate the intricacies of the LBW rule, which has baffled everyone, including the *cognoscenti*, whilst nevertheless pursuing his interest in the peaceful settlement of international disputes.

The Hague Academy of International Law and the Development of the Settlement of Disputes as a Global Mechanism

Yves Daudet*

I must say first of all how pleased and honoured I am to have been invited to be a speaker during this day of tributes to Steven van Hoogstraten, who for many years was in charge of this Palace devoted to the settlement of disputes, the promotion of peace and the development of international law. Having worked alongside Steven van Hoogstraten in his capacity as Treasurer of The Hague Academy of International Law for 10 years, I can bear witness to his interest – which is often passionate – for these questions. He rarely missed the reading of a Judgment of the Court, and often attended the Academy's courses, which provided food for his thinking in these fields, which are embodied here in the Peace Palace, of which he was a very attentive Director.

Although jurisprudence and doctrine are not the main sources of international law, they serve as pillars of reference, and are broadly determinative for the development of this discipline. The ICJ is the highest international court, the PCA is the matrix for arbitration, and the Academy is one of the main crucibles for the development of doctrine. These three institutions exist side-by-side in these premises, and are a leading centre for the settlement of disputes and the study of dispute settlement.

Within this institutional whole, the Academy of International Law plays a specific role, in the sense that the nature of its devotion to the settlement of disputes is not the same as that of the Court or the PCA, whose very mission or, in other words, whose *raison d'être*, is the settlement of disputes.

* Former Secretary-General of The Hague Academy of International Law. At present President of the Curatorium of The Hague Academy.

Indeed, when I refer to the activities of the Academy and to the foremost of such activities, which is teaching and research in public and private international law, it is quite clear that not all of its courses and researches are devoted to the settlement of disputes as such, even though some of them are, such as those dealing with arbitration, for example. On the other hand, however, it is very rare that a course does not incorporate this aspect, through an analysis of the jurisprudence arising out of disputes relating to the issues under examination.

But this is not where the essential differences and specificities of approach lie. The vision one may have and the analysis of the question of dispute settlement are not at all the same, depending on whether they are viewed from the perspective of the ICJ or any other Tribunal as well as the parties, on the one hand, or from the perspective of the Academy and of doctrinal authorities on the other hand.

To be rather schematic, I would say that what is expected of the Court is that it should exercise its function which, to use the words of Article 38 of its Statute, is "to decide in accordance with international law such disputes as are submitted to it". To decide disputes. And so, in what I would dare to call the chronology of interest in the decision that is handed down, States and their counsel are primarily interested in the last part of the judgment, the "ruling", which tells them whether the Court agrees with them or not. Doctrinal authorities and the Academy are primarily interested in the ground and the thought process that has led to the particular solution. These are the rules and principles that have been applied and the jurisprudence that has been established or confirmed or, on rare occasions, modified.

As for the Court, it pays the greatest attention to the way in which it formulates its reasons, because it knows the use to which these reasons may subsequently be put, the risks for the future that might arise out of one formulation or another, and the interpretation that will be put on this formulation by analysts and commentators. Nevertheless, the Court, which applies international law, does not seek to "make" international law. The Court does not act as a "law maker" and does not seek to do so. However, in spite of itself, if I may say so, the positions that it takes and the reasons that it gives are always also moments of "interpretation" and sometimes of "creation" of law, and it is then for the Academy to take over and interest itself in this. Indeed, it is for a large part through the jurisprudence that international law can develop and, above all, develop with a certain consistency. And so the Academy's courses are devoted to analysing these trends, which are like a groundswell, and these courses seek in turn to uncover the backbone of international law, as it can be discerned from the thought processes of the judge, together with the opinions that may be appended to the judgment.

In the context of an evolving international law where voluntarism is losing its place to objectivism, it is clear that the role of the judge grows when he acknowledges the existence and states the scope of objective rules, of rules that are applicable *erga omnes*, or even of *jus cogens*, thus contributing to the establishment of an organized "legal order" – in fact I am tempted to say a "rule of international law" in the same way as we speak of a "rule of law" in municipal law.

I do believe that this general and all-encompassing analysis of general international law is necessary if we are not to fall into the trap of fragmentation or confine ourselves to narrow specializations. In this regard, I believe that the Academy plays an essential role. The General Courses delivered in Public on Private International Law are aiming at such a global analysis.

I will now switch to French.

M'exprimer en français est pour moi une facilité dont je ne me cache pas, mais c'est aussi une occasion de rappeler que Steven a une parfaite maîtrise de cette langue dont il connaît toutes les subtilités et idiomes. C'est donc une autre manière de lui rendre hommage.

L'Académie, dans les cours qu'y dispensent les professeurs invités, ne connaît aucune des contraintes du juge, qu'elles soient procédurales ou de fond. Point de compromis auquel elle devrait se tenir, de demande qui limiterait ses actions, de jurisprudence dont elle pourrait très difficilement s'écarter. Si deux tribunaux de l'ordre interne décident différemment dans des espèces semblables, c'est un problème nécessitant qu'une haute juridiction dise la ligne à suivre ce qui se produit sans difficultés dans l'ordre interne mais n'est pas si simple à concevoir dans l'ordre international, tout particulièrement aujourd'hui où l'on assiste à une multiplication des juridictions internationales. Si deux professeurs expriment des points de vue différents, ce n'est nullement un problème, c'est un «débat doctrinal», recherché et encouragé et à juste titre considéré comme fécond pour une formation accomplie des futurs juristes.

L'analyse des différends et de leur règlement est donc particulièrement souhaitable en ce qu'elle est le meilleur exercice permettant de comprendre que le droit n'est pas univoque et que le principe du contradictoire n'est pas seulement une règle de procédure applicable dans les prétoires permettant un procès équitable, mais aussi une méthode d'analyse de fond utilisée à l'Académie comme dans les universités. Je pense que le rôle de l'Académie dans cette entreprise de mise en lumière de toutes les facettes des questions et d'apprentissage de la variété des approches pour les traiter est dans une situation particulièrement privilégiée.

L'ouverture internationale qu'elle réalise avec près de cent nationalités différentes qui y sont représentées dans les cours d'été et bientôt dans ceux d'hiver – c'est l'occasion pour moi d'annoncer ici une étape importante dans son développement – contraint à la prise en compte des éléments culturels et sociologiques ajoutés aux analyses juridiques et bien des cours, délivrés par de grands noms du droit international, ont parfaitement atteint cet objectif et ont pu montrer que, en particulier et notamment, les questions de règlement des différends ne sont pas nécessairement traitées de manière univoque. En même temps, dès lors qu'il s'agit de paix et de règlement des différends, il est certain qu'une culture doit être impérativement développée. Les lieux où nous nous trouvons aujourd'hui y sont incontestablement propices. Ils invitent à y instituer des réflexes de paix et de règlement pacifique des différends. Je dis bien des réflexes au sens d'une conduite automatique dans une direction vers laquelle on est naturellement porté. Dans ce temps où des terroristes sont à nos portes et souvent hélas les franchissent, le renforcement d'une culture de paix et de règlement pacifique des différends est une ardente obligation. L'Académie s'y essaye et souvent avec succès : j'ai le souvenir, lors du conflit opposant la Russie à la Géorgie au cours de l'été 2008, d'étudiants russes et géorgiens de l'Académie s'installant autour d'une table pour conduire un dialogue constructif de ce que pourrait être, de ce que devrait être, le retour à la paix. J'ai aussi le souvenir d'étudiants égyptiens et israéliens qui avaient tant étonné leurs camarades qui observaient leur recherche apaisée et responsable des moyens par lesquels cette terre de conflits pourrait être celle du lait et du miel. Dans l'auditorium de l'Académie se trouvent chaque année de futurs responsables nationaux et internationaux. Qu'ils aient acquis de tels réflexes et soient portés à adopter de tels comportement porte à l'optimisme pour notre futur.

En vous disant que l'apprentissage et la diffusion d'une culture du règlement pacifique des conflits, comme l'Académie s'y emploie, constituent une grande partie du chemin vers un monde apaisé, vous considérerez sans doute que je tiens un langage de professeur français légèrement décalé des réalités. Peut être… mais moi je ne le pense pas ! Vous conviendrez avec moi que les plus grands malheurs de l'humanité sont les fruits de l'ignorance et de l'obscurantisme. Quoi de plus dramatiquement absurde que l'antisémitisme qui est un aveuglement ou l'amalgame entre l'Islam, religion de paix, et l'islamisme radical entreprise de destruction pour prendre deux exemples d'une triste actualité. L'Académie a son rôle à jouer en exposant les fondements culturels des règles juridiques qui nous gouvernent et il en va du droit international comme des autres branches du droit. La spécificité du droit international d'aujourd'hui est qu'il déploie ses effets dans un monde globalisé, plus globalisé qu'il ne le fut jamais dans l'histoire de l'humanité. L'Académie s'efforce de contribuer à cette diffusion du droit international. Steven van Hoogstraten l'avait bien analysé et y a contribué, nous lui devons donc beaucoup de gratitude. Mais j'observe que les fonctions de Trésorier de l'Académie sont marquées par une forme de continuité et, dans cette journée d'hommage envers lui, Steven comprendra certainement que je sois heureux d'observer chez son successeur, Erik de Baedts, le même intérêt que celui qui était le sien pour les activités de l'Académie en me réjouissant de poursuivre une coopération fructueuse entre le Trésorier et le Secrétaire général de l'Académie de droit international de La Haye, Capitale si bien choisie du droit international.

The Constitutional Role of the ICJ within the UN System

Niels Blokker*

Excellencies,

Ladies and Gentlemen, Dear Steven,

I greatly appreciate the invitation to speak at this farewell seminar in honour of Steven van Hoogstraten. The organizers have given me an impossible task: to talk about a broad, important and complex topic but to do so for only ten minutes. The topic is "the constitutional role of the ICJ". I will try to make my task manageable, speak a bit *staccato*, and hope we can go into more detail in the discussion.

My topic is mainly about the question whether or to what extent judicial review should be possible of acts of some of the organs of the United Nations, in particular the Security Council, the General Assembly and the Secretariat. I will briefly discuss three questions:

Is there a need for such judicial review? My answer is "yes".

Since there is such a need, I will look at this from the perspective of the key question of this seminar: "Is the Peace Palace still at the heart of international dispute settlement?" My answer is "no".

Is it necessary for the ICJ to play a more prominent role in this area? My answer is "yes".

I will now briefly explain these questions and my answers.

1

So my first question is: is there a need for judicial review of acts of UN organs?

* Professor of International Institutional Law at the Grotius Centre for International Legal Studies of Leiden University.

If we look at past practice, it is clear that increasingly a need is felt to scrutinize acts of some of the organs of the UN. Let me briefly mention some examples.

In the 1990s, a strong need was felt to review the lawfulness of the creation by the Security Council of the ICTY and the ICTR. Already at the creation of these criminal tribunals, the lawfulness of their creation was questioned by some of the members of the Council (e.g. China and Brazil). Therefore, it did not come as a surprise when, in the very first case before the ICTY, *Tadić*, the defence filed a preliminary motion claiming that the Security Council did not have the competence to create the ICTY. The Trial Chamber concluded in August 1995 in half a page that the ICTY was not "a constitutional court set up to scrutinize the actions of organs of the United Nations" and therefore could not review the resolution establishing the Tribunal. However, at the same time it rightly perceived an immense need to address this question. Therefore, somewhat contradictory, the Trial Chamber in fact scrutinized the Security Council decision in the remainder of its decision. Three months later, the Appeals Chamber of the ICTY, under the presidency of Antonio Cassese, disagreed fundamentally with the Trial Chamber and concluded that the ICTY is competent to decide whether or not it was lawfully created. But this is not the end of the story. In 2012 the Special Tribunal for Lebanon decided in the *Ayyash* case that it lacked the authority to review the relevant Security Council resolution. Therefore : the law is unsettled on this. But it is clear that there was a need for judicial review of the relevant Security Council decisions.

My next example relates to individual financial sanctions that have been imposed by the Security Council since the late 1990s in a number of situations. This instrument was used in particular against hundreds of individuals associated with Al Qaida. However, some of these individuals claimed that they were not at all associated with Al Qaida. All they could do was to address the same sanctions committee that had put them on the list, requesting to be removed from the list. The individuals concerned did not have any legal remedy at all. Soon they started to bring cases before a number of national and international courts, not only claiming that they were not associated with Al Qaida, but also that they did not have a legal remedy. Most famous are the *Kadi* cases. Increasingly a strong need was felt to review the relevant decisions by the SC and its sanction committees. Over the years the Security Council has to some extent remedied this deficiency, by creating an independent Ombudsperson. But this has not satisfied the EU Court of Justice.

Third example: in 2010 the ICC Review Conference reached agreement on the crime of aggression. The future rules for the exercise of jurisdiction over this crime provide for judicial review by the ICC of decisions by the Security Council that an act of aggression has been committed. The delicacy of this is reflected in the wording of the relevant provision of the Kampala amendments: "A determination of an act of aggression by an organ outside the Court shall be without prejudice to the Court's own findings under this Statute" (Art. 15*bis* 9 = Art. 15*ter* 4).

A final example concerns findings by the Secretary-General of the UN that certain acts performed by UN staff or experts on mission are official acts for which they enjoy immunity from jurisdiction. If this leads to a dispute, the relevant State may bring the matter before the ICJ under Section 30 of the UN General Convention. This happened in the late 1990s in the *Cumaraswamy* case. In this case there was a sort of "review lite" by the Court. It was of the opinion "that the Secretary-General correctly found that Mr. Cumaraswamy[, in speaking the words quoted in the a rticle in International Commercial Litigation,] was acting in the course of the performance of his mission as Special Rapporteur".

It is clear from these examples that the need has arisen in practice to scrutinize acts of UN organs. More in general, this seems to occur in at least two types of situations. First of all: since the 1990s the Security Council has used more intensively the considerable powers given to it by the Charter. This has triggered the need for checks and balances. Secondly, the need to review may correspond to the right to a remedy for individuals. This right is recognized in all major international human rights instruments. Why should individuals only have this right in relation to measures taken by states, affecting them directly, and not in relation to similar measures taken by UN organs?

2

This brings me to my second question. Since there is an increased need to scrutinize acts of UN organs, let us look at this from the perspective of the key question of this seminar: "Is the Peace Palace still at the heart of international dispute settlement?"

On this, I can be very brief. Whenever in practice acts of UN organs were scrutinized, the scrutinizer normally was not one of the inhabitants of the Peace Palace, but rather other international courts and tribunals as well as national courts.

3

Finally, I will address a third question: is it necessary for the ICJ to play a more prominent role in this area? My answer is "yes".

Whenever judicial review of acts of UN organs is necessary, such review by national courts or by international courts other than the ICJ often has disadvantages.

National courts by definition will carry out the review from their own national perspective, not from the international perspective from which the reviewed act originates.

And there is the danger of fragmentation: different national courts may take fundamentally different review decisions, undermining the unity of international law.

Review by international courts does not have these disadvantages. But it is only the ICJ that has a general universal jurisdiction. The jurisdiction of other international courts is limited to certain regions of the world or to a specialized area of international law, such as international criminal law or human rights.

Therefore, there is a need for the ICJ to play a strong role in this area, in order to maintain and strengthen the authority of organs of the UN and the coherence of international law. If there is the real possibility for the ICJ to scrutinize decisions of UN organs, this will reduce some of the pressure on other international courts and tribunals as well as national courts to step in, to act as second-best, "substitute reviewers".

At present, other international courts and tribunals as well as national courts may find themselves in the position that if they do not review, light or full, nobody will do it. This is a result that many national or international judges will find unacceptable, as it is against the rule of law, a denial of justice. It takes away checks and balances, and it may leave complainants without a remedy.

This was emphasized by the ICTY Trial Chamber (para. 6). Even though the Trial Chamber stated that it was not "a constitutional court set up to scrutinize the actions of organs of the United Nations", scrutinizing the action of the SC was precisely what it did. Why? "[A] body that judges the criminality of this behaviour should be viewed as legitimate. This is the first time that the international community has created a court with criminal jurisdiction. The establishment of the International Tribunal has now spawned the creation of an *ad hoc* Tribunal for Rwanda. Each of these *ad hoc* Tribunals represents an important step towards the establishment of a permanent international criminal tribunal. In this context, the Trial Chamber considers that it would be inappropriate to dismiss without comment the accused's contentions that the establishment of the International Tribunal by the Security Council was beyond power and an ill-founded political action, not reasonably aimed at restoring and maintaining peace, and that the International Tribunal is not duly established by law."

In 2009 the Canadian federal Court criticized the lack of remedies in the UN Al Qaida financial individual sanctions, and compared the situation of someone on a UN financial sanctions list "not unlike that of Josef K. in Kafka's *The Trial*, who awakes one morning, and for reasons never revealed to him or the reader, is arrested and prosecuted for an unspecified crime".

A more pronounced role for the ICJ in this area would also be welcome because the views of national and/or other international courts may vary widely. As a result, the law is unsettled. In such cases, the ICJ is best placed to improve the situation. An example are the decisions of the ICTY Appeals Chamber in *Tadić* and of the Special Tribunal for Lebanon in *Ayyash*. Basically the STL concluded that it lacked the authority to review the relevant SC resolution, whereas the ICTY had concluded earlier that such an authority is part of the Tribunal's inherent jurisdiction.

If the ICJ would play a more prominent role in this area, it would be easier for national courts and other international courts and tribunals to be less engaged in this field, to exercise more restraint.

In this context a final question may be whether the ICJ is indeed suitable to play such a more prominent role. One way to answer this question is by analysing the track record of the ICJ in this area. The main decisions in which the Court has scrutinized decisions of UN organs are, in staccato: *IMCO – Composition of the Maritime Safety Committee* (1960), *Certain Expenses* (1962), *Namibia* (1971), *WHO Nuclear Weapons* (1996), *Mazilu* (1989), *Cumaraswamy*

(1999). No time is left to go into more detail here. But I would take the position that, in general, the Court has proceeded with the necessary caution in this field. It has fully played its role as a judicial body, a court of law, while also taking into account political sensitivities, not being deaf to political reality. In all the cases I just mentioned, the Court has developed the notion of "practice of the organization", as a legal technique to confirm its legal arguments but also as a reality check.

Mediation as an Alternative for International Dispute Settlement

Jeroen Vervliet*

A. Introduction

My assignment for today is to speak about mediation. I have wholeheartedly accepted the request to address you, Steven, and I have deliberately selected this mediation topic in the array of potential subjects.

Whilst speaking about mediation, I equally benefit from the opportunity to tailor my words and reflect upon your career in the Peace Palace as General Director and as Treasurer of The Hague Academy of International Law.

B. Why not The Hague?

Steven, you have always lived up to the idea of adding an extra, new promising activity to the Peace Palace, to develop a platform for Peace Talks. Why Geneva or Oslo, why Camp David and Dayton? Why not The Hague?

The Hague has got its extraordinary history, the 1st and 2nd Hague Peace Conferences of 1899 and 1907. The Peace Palace as authoritative symbol of Peace, Peace through Justice, Peace and International Law. And all other institutions that have come in its slipstream.

For what reason has The Hague failed in acquiring the name and fame of a successful city for Peace Talks, where parties enjoy the good circumstances of safety and confidentiality? I think it is because of the formal phenomenon of the Law.

* Peace Palace Library Director, which is part of the Carnegie Foundation. President of the International Association of Law Libraries (IALL).

Does the Law, and the Law's strict reasoning, establish the idea that The Hague – symbolizing Arbitration and Adjudication – cannot sufficiently guarantee freedom and creativity, distinction and sovereignty, contrary to mediation.

C. Article 98 of the UN Charter. Mediation. Cyprus

Still, we, you and I, have witnessed and even participated in high-level Peace Talks. In March 2003, Kofi Annan had convened all parties in the Cyprus Peace Negotations.

According to the United Nations website – as stated in the United Nations Charter, Art. 98 – the Secretary- General "shall perform such other functions as are entrusted to him by these organs", that is to say, particularly the General Assembly or the Security Council. These other functions often include functions in the field of the prevention and the peaceful settlement of disputes, especially so-called good offices and mediation. This mediation role of the Secretary-General has been developed through extensive practice and can be set in motion at the Secretary-General's own initiative.

Thus, in March 2003, Kofi Annan did so in his capacity of mediator, a special role for the Secretary-General of the United Nations. I will come back to this special UN-SG mediator role.

D. What is Mediation?

But, what is mediation? To what extent does it differ from negotiations, good offices etc.? How does it relate to arbitration and adjudication?

Mediation is a means to unravel a conflict in the arena of politics and diplomacy, involving the assistance of a third party, is (always) characterized by its non-binding and (mostly) non-legal nature. Contrary to arbitration and adjudication.

Article 33 (1) of the Charter of the United Nations cites the various mechanisms for the peaceful settlement of international disputes: negotiation, enquiry, mediation, arbitration, judicial settlement etc., as if we have to deal with a tiered constellation or a certain hierarchy.

The 1899 Convention for the Pacific Settlement of International Disputes, giving birth to the PCA, mentions the non-legal modality of mediation to be pursued by friendly Powers before an appeal to arms or during the course of a conflict (Art. 2 and Art. 3).

E. Definition

- Mediation is a flexible but structured voluntary endeavour in which the consent of parties is essential.
- The mediation, a third party intervention, is guided by an impartial neutral authoritative person or organization of integrity.
- The mediator must be experienced, well-prepared and well-informed about/well-introduced in the dispute.
- The mediator shapes, for the benefit of an effective outcome, an atmosphere of confidentiality.
- The mediator guarantees a fair and balanced and just treatment and process.
- The mediator's aim is to end disruptive behaviour, liberating parties out of a mutually hurting stalemate, avoid war (international or civil), establish ceasefire, reach peace agreements and stop the escalation of a costly conflict, and after investigating – the diagnosis – and defining the dispute – the formulation –, and handing in recommendations, mutually acceptable for both parties – in which concessions are made –, the mediator comes to compensating measures and constructs the peaceful settlement of international disputes, i.e. preventive diplomacy, peacemaking, peacekeeping and peacebuilding.

- The mediator approaches both parties symmetrically and as equals in the conflict to be resolved.
- The role or mandate of the mediator needs to be clear for both parties.
- This clarity is important for the viable and durable outcome.

Conditions, which are, at least in my view, very much similar to the formulation of the classic *compromis*.

- The mediator is a facilitator, formulator and manipulator.
- Thus, mediation is not a series of *ad hoc* diplomatic negotations.
- Negotiations are dyadic, mediation is a triadic structure. Mediation is nevertheless a subset of negotiation.
- It happens sometimes that third parties offer their mediation services, with the objective to extend their influence, e.g. States use mediation as a foreign policy instrument.

Briefly. The currently well-accepted condition is that a successful mediation involves an undisputed and authoritative person (or organization) of a supra-national kind, e.g. – today – the Secretary-General of the United Nations; or another individual or representative of an international organization examplifying impartiality, leverage (exerting influence or power) and having status.

In the past, – because it is all about authority – for instance in the Middle Ages, crowned heads of states, such as kings, or representatives appointed by them, or church officials, such as popes and priests, gave awards.

And what is Apollo's response received from the Delphi oracle, embodied by Hugo Grotius, the founder of Modern International Law, in *De Iure Belli ac Pacis ("On the laws of War and Peace")*, the ultimate anchorage for persuasive legal reasoning? What is Grotius' authoritative, wise and prophetic opinion or statement as an answer to our consultation request?

I intentionally and calculatingly hope to discover a key, because you, Steven, have always encouraged me to expand the Special and

Rare Hugo Grotius Collection in the Peace Palace Library, although you still kept your critical considerations about the value thereof and struggled with the nowadays virtue of the historic content of Hugo Grotius' works.

In Book 2, Chapter 23 "On the Dubious Causes of War", Paragraph 8 "Not declaring War, For This May Be Avoided by Arbitration, Hugo Grotius mentions arbitration as a means to prevent war, in addition to the value of conference for the avoidance of a war. Hugo Grotius refers to Priests in the past and to Kings in his epoch having the duty to prevent warfare by acting as arbitrating umpires, and thus assisting in avoiding inconvenience, such as war, and obliging to accept peace upon fair and reasonable terms.

In Book 3, Chapter 20 "Finishing of a War", Paragraph 56 "War Ended by Arbitration, Without Appeal" and Paragraph 57 "Arbiters Bound to Equity in Doubtful Cases", Hugo Grotius cites two sorts of arbitrations; the first type of arbitration being of a rather absolute character, operating on the basis of a *compromis*, issuing sentences which must be obeyed, whether just or unjust, without appeal, since the king and his nation have concluded a *compromis*, and there is no superior power over the king or a sovereign state; the second kind of arbitration is characterized by the honest and equitable effect of a judgment, and he calls it mediation.

F. *Beagle Channel* Case. A Successful Mediation

In the Peace Palace you can find the bust of the British King Edward VII, who led the 1902 arbitration between Argentina and Chile.

At the beginning of the 20th century, Pope Leo XIII pleaded for peace and for devotion to Christ the Redeemer. At the same time, Argentina and Chile were almost at arms over the common frontier. As a mark of the peaceful settlement of their international dispute a huge Cristo Redentor, the original, was erected high in the Andes mountains. You can find a small-scale copy of Cristo Redentor, in front of the Japanese Room.

Steven, you have co-organized the External Programme of The Hague Academy of International Law, visiting in two subsequent years, first Chile and then Argentina.

Therefore I have decided to treat the *Beagle Channel* case. Scholars always refer to the *Beagle Channel* case as the most successful mediation. Its history mirrors almost all instruments of peaceful settlement of international disputes. Still, mediation offered the solution.

In 1977, arbitrators of the International Court of Justice gathered in a panel appointed by Queen Elizabeth II delivered an award, that happened to be too controversial and unacceptable for Argentina; it concerned an arbitration resulting out of and in accordance with the 1902 Treaty, that was denounced by Argentina in the meantime for its arbitration outcome. So, Argentina rejected the award in early 1978, whilst Chile centred on the respect for the decision taken.

Hereupon a negotiation started but failed. Argentina was certainly heading for war, the navies of Chile and Argentina were on the brink of a sea battle in the Strait of Magellan, near Cape Horn, – ripeness of the conflict (in terminology of mediation), a condition for embarking upon a mediation – but the very launch of military attacks was almost divinely prevented because a vehement tempest was raging; the start of the war was impossible.

Pope John Paul II offered "good offices", in bringing the parties back to the negotiation table. Thereafter more active involvement, the mediation by the Vatican under the auspices of the Pope, started, all led by Cardinal Antonio Samoré. The proceedings followed a rather strict structure.

Samoré first gathered information and heard both parties (diagnosis), then set an agenda (formulation), searched for elements in the controversy about which concession could be achieved, what compensations could be given during the process and how the agreement could be constructed. Samoré's mediation confirmed the sovereignty of Chile over the disputed islands, but in return Chile relinquished its claims on South Atlantic waters, and Argentina retained its maritime rights.

It was merely the lack of territorial or military interest of the Church, its objectivity and impartiality, the Catholic character of both countries and the Papal involvement in South America during five centuries, ever since the Treaty of Tordesillas, that shaped the moral authority of the Pope to successfully lead the mediation; also because peace is not only a political issue but a spiritual state as well. Trust was a key notion.

Three times Chile invited Argentina to submit the dispute to the International Court of Justice. Unsuccessfully, for Argentina had little faith or appetite in juridical dealings after the award of Queen Elizabeth II. It would also endanger the mediation outcome. Argentina even considered the submission itself a *"casus belli"*. By the way, what would have been the position of the International Court of Justice, having cooperated in an arbitration, and an award given that had been rejected? Eventually, a successful mediation was settled in 1984; succesful because peace was maintained in rough political times and a durable peace has been established.

For me personally, it is highly interesting that Cardinal Antonio Samoré was by then the Head Librarian and Chief Archivist of the Vatican, apparently a capacity to act neutrally, be well-informed and working systematically, embodying confidentiality, and his characteristics – extremely patient, taking his time to solve the problem with the necessary sophistication – are said to have been instrumental for the success.

G. Ban Ki-moon and Mediation

On the centenary day of the Peace Palace, 28 August 2013, the United Nations Secretary-General Ban Ki- moon, said: "give peace a chance". And: "give diplomacy a chance", as he was speaking on Syria, "the biggest challenge for war and peace today".

In 2012 United Nations Secretary-General Ban Ki-moon published a report (A/66/811) under the self-explanatory title "Strengthening the Role of Mediation in the Peaceful Settlement of Disputes, Conflict Prevention and Resolution".

This document was preceded by a resolution of the United Nations General Assembly (A/65/283), in which mediation was mentioned as one of the instruments of peaceful settlement of international disputes, in conformity with Article 33 (1) of the United Nations Charter, and that mediation very much upholds and respects the sovereignty and equality of States; the resolution recognizes "the increased use of mediation" and calls "on key actors to develop their mediation capacities".

This as a follow-up to the 2009 report of the Secretary-General on "Enhancing Mediation and Its Support Activities" (S/2009/189) examining the mediation challenges faced by the United Nations.

Therefore a guidance for more effective mediation was requested, also contributing to professionalism. Thus, the so-called "Guidance for Effective Mediation", dating from 2012, disseminated by the Mediation Support Unit of the Department of Political Affairs of the United Nations, a service provider assisting in and facilitating mediation, and a mediation knowledge repository.

H. New Role for The Hague

The question arises whether mediation is only the second-best vehicle for pacific dispute settlement, or has mediation – in comparison to arbitration and adjudication – over time succeeded to prove to be equally effective, and binding or (morally) binding upon the parties? Could the Peace Palace, the symbol of Peace through Justice, open its doors for a permanent mediation centre?

The Hague, the Legal Capital of the World, carries in its coat of arms *"De Stad van Recht en Vrede"*. And although Law is receiving a lot of emphasis, we know perfectly well that Peace could also be achieved in a non-legal way. Law might bring parties in juxtaposition, whereas mediation, as a species of negotiation, is not specifically reasoning according to the Law, and that delivers a 21st century liberty to creatively find peaceful settlements of international disputes.

Do we jeopardize the Peace Palace as an icon? The Peace Palace is very much associated with Peace through Justice, and identified as the home of the United Nations World Court, the International Court of Justice.

Could the Peace Palace, therefore, as easily be perceived as the international mediation centre? And . . . thus fulfil the instrumentalization requirements of Ban Ki-moon's mediation policy?

Yes. The Peace Palace is unique, houses a number of authoritative institutions that have a profound knowledge of conflict resolution, that can equally support mediation, and the Peace Palace is an international symbol of peace, a safe haven and neutral location, that radiates confidence. By adding this new function of mediation, in the shape of an international mediation platform, to the array of business deployed in the Peace Palace, the Peace Palace will get a modern political and active platform in the service of Peace.

Steven, thanks for the years in which we have worked together.

Vers une nouvelle philosophie pour la justice pénale internationale

François Roux*

Après avoir représenté un immense progrès, après avoir suscité tant d'espoirs, la justice pénale internationale traverse une période de sévère remise en question.

Si comme le dit le philosophe français Edgar Morin, «… toute crise est ambivalente. En même temps que des forces régressives ou désintégratrices, les forces génératrices créatrices s'éveillent souvent dans les crises»[1], alors vive la crise de la justice pénale internationale.

Nous nous proposons d'identifier ici les difficultés rencontrées à ce jour et de proposer, à l'occasion de cette crise d'adolescence, les solutions trop longtemps repoussées.

A. De la lutte *contre* l'impunité à la lutte pour la justice, ou comment donner à la défense sa juste place dans la justice pénale internationale

1. Défendre celui qui est accusé d'avoir commis l'indéfendable, l'irréparable, l'insoutenable

Au début étaient les principes de la nécessaire lutte contre l'impunité énoncés par l'immense expert que fût aux Nations Unies, Louis Joinet.

C'est grâce à ces principes que se sont créées les premières juridictions pénales internationales, d'abord très inspirées de cette

* Avocat Honoraire, Chef du Bureau de la défense, Tribunal spécial pour le Liban (jusque mars 2018). Dernier ouvrage paru: *Justice internationale, La parole est à la défense.*

1. *Le Monde*, 3 septembre 2014, «Inventer une sociologie du présent».

mission au point que la place de la défense y fût tout juste tolérée comme un mal nécessaire…

Or, comme tout citoyen, tout avocat est choqué, révolté par les images de crimes de masse, de génocide, de terrorisme, et sa compassion va bien évidemment immédiatement aux victimes.

Mais, dès lors qu'une personne est accusée de ces crimes, est arrêtée et traduite devant un tribunal, l'honneur de l'avocat est de mettre sa robe, de se lever, et de défendre.

C'est aussi évident que cela.

Très vite les avocats commis d'office devant les juridictions pénales internationales ont fait leur travail, celui de défendre. Quelle que soit la gravité du crime reproché.

> «Défendre, c'est ne rien accepter pour acquis, qui n'ait été soumis au crible de la critique» disait l'avocat Maître Jean Boudot.[2]»

Est-ce un hasard si beaucoup de ces avocats venaient d'ONG des droits de l'homme, faisant leurs les propos de François Zimmeray ancien Ambassadeur français pour les droits de l'homme «les droits de l'homme sont par nature, un droit de victimes, mais c'est dans la défense des accusés, fussent-ils coupables, qu'ils trouvent leur application la plus élevée»?

Adoptant la philosophie de la Croix-Rouge selon laquelle «quand un ennemi est blessé, ce n'est plus un ennemi mais un homme à soigner», les avocats considèrent que quand un homme est accusé, menotté, emprisonné, ce n'est plus un ennemi, c'est un homme à défendre.

Et c'est bien là la mission première de l'avocat: d'abord rencontrer un homme. L'avocat est toujours le témoin privilégié et déchiré, de l'humanité de tout homme, même accusé des pires crimes.

---

2. *Le Monde*, 15 mai 2013.

«Monsieur le Président, depuis que j'ai vu l'homme derrière le bourreau... et qu'il me ressemble, je ne m'en sors plus» disait devant les Chambres extraordinaires auprès des tribunaux cambodgiens (CETC), au procès de Douch, ancien Directeur de la sinistre prison S 21 au Cambodge, François Bizot qui fût son prisonnier et en a écrit un témoignage bouleversant dans son livre *Le portail*.

L'avocat de l'extrême, celui qui se confronte dans les tribunaux pénaux internationaux aux plus grands crimes, fait l'expérience de cet abîme.

Il va pourtant, patiemment, professionnellement, éthiquement, reprendre les éléments du dossier, les confronter à la critique comme le dit Jean Boudot et les soumettre au Juge, souvent en le surprenant. Car c'est son métier de surprendre, de soulever des points que personne n'a voulu voir et qui existent pourtant, dans le dossier comme dans le contexte.

Ce faisant, l'avocat exercera la défense. Non pas seulement comme une fin en soi, mais comme une œuvre de justice. Il devra le faire avec excellence car le jugement de ces tragédies nécessite un énorme travail, de grandes compétences professionnelles et déontologiques, et beaucoup de discernement, pour appréhender un contexte culturel, sociologique, communautaire, politique voire géopolitique tout à fait nouveau, pour lui comme pour tous les acteurs du procès pénal international.

Point de lutte *contre l'impunité* dans tout cela, mais bien de lutte *pour la justice*. «Seulement» et pleinement la recherche de la vérité et de la justice, pour les victimes, pour l'accusé, et au-delà pour des communautés affectées, traumatisées, qui ont le droit de savoir et qui ne pourront se reconstruire qu'à travers un procès qui aura respecté les standards et les normes les plus élevés.

Les avocats n'ont donc pas part à la lutte contre l'impunité. Celle-ci relève du seul Procureur.

Les avocats devant les juridictions pénales internationales ont part à la lutte pour la justice après les grandes tragédies humaines. Comme le dit la Cour européenne des droits de l'homme dans l'arrêt *Morice c. France*, les avocats sont «des acteurs de justice»[3]. Par leur engagement, par leur contribution à l'établissement de la vérité, au moins judiciaire, peut-être historique, les avocats participent ainsi eux aussi à la construction de la paix par la justice. J'affirme ici que les avocats sont à la justice internationale ce que les casques bleus sont au maintien de la paix: indispensables.

Ainsi, à partir du moment où l'on crée des juridictions pénales internationales, où l'on installe des Procureurs pour poursuivre les personnes suspectées de crimes les plus graves, et des juges pour les juger, que serait un procès sans avocat de la défense?

2. Inscrire la défense dans le paysage de la justice pénale internationale

«Il ne peut pas y avoir de justice pénale internationale sans une défense forte» disait le Procureur Richard Golstone.

Et pourtant depuis le début des juridictions pénales internationales, la défense est le parent pauvre de cette justice.

Pourquoi? Parce que comme dit ci-dessus les juges restent trop souvent prisonniers des raisons pour lesquelles la communauté internationale crée ces juridictions «pour lutter contre l'impunité». La conséquence est que le châtiment des personnes accusées devient la priorité. Alors une défense? Pour quoi faire?

Certes il en faut bien une pour que le décor de justice soit parfait, mais de là à lui donner des moyens et du pouvoir…

C'est oublier que devant les deux Tribunaux internationaux de l'ex-Yougoslavie et du Rwanda, prés de 25 % des personnes mises

3. *Morice c. France*, CEDH, Arrêt de la Grande Chambre, 23 avril 2015, requête n° 29369/10.

en accusation ont ensuite été déclarées «non coupables». Erreurs du Procureur? Fausses accusations de témoins? Quoiqu'il en soit c'est parce qu'une défense sérieuse, compétente, efficace malgré les difficultés, a fait son travail, que 25 % d'erreurs judiciaires ont été évitées.

Ceci rappelle simplement que le rôle premier des juges n'est pas de lutter contre l'impunité mais de rendre la justice après avoir entendu contradictoirement l'accusation et la défense.

Combien de fois ai-je dit aux juges: «S'il est vrai que nos juridictions sont instituées par la communauté internationale pour lutter contre l'impunité, ce qui est une noble intention à laquelle nous ne pouvons tous qu'adhérer, une fois qu'elles sont créées et que vous êtes nommés, vous devez vous défaire de cette notion à l'origine de votre nomination. Vous n'êtes pas en croisade contre l'impunité. Le seul qui est là pour lutter contre l'impunité, c'est le Procureur. Quant à vous vous êtes là pour dire si oui ou non le Procureur a rapporté la preuve que la personne qui est accusée a commis les faits qu'on lui reproche. Et vous ne pourrez juger de cela qu'après avoir entendu, contradictoirement l'accusation et la défense».

Et je leur cite souvent le magnifique texte, quasi spirituel, que le président de la cour d'assises lit aux jurés avant d'entrer en salle de délibérations, l'article 353 du Code de procédure pénale français:

> «Avant que la cour d'assises se retire, le président donne lecture de l'instruction suivante, qui est, en outre, affichée en gros caractères, dans le lieu le plus apparent de la chambre des délibérations:
> Sous réserve de l'exigence de motivation de la décision, la loi ne demande pas compte à chacun des juges et jurés composant la cour d'assises des moyens par lesquels ils se sont convaincus, elle ne leur prescrit pas de règles desquelles ils doivent faire particulièrement dépendre la plénitude et

> la suffisance d'une preuve; elle leur prescrit de s'interroger eux-mêmes dans le silence et le recueillement et de chercher, dans la sincérité de leur conscience, quelle impression ont faite, sur leur raison, les preuves rapportées contre l'accusé, et les moyens de sa défense. La loi ne leur fait que cette seule question, qui renferme toute la mesure de leurs devoirs: «Avez-vous une intime conviction?»

Le droit de la *common law* indique quant à lui que le Procureur doit rapporter la preuve de la culpabilité de l'accusé au-delà de tout doute raisonnable, ce qui est une autre manière de dire la même chose.

C'est donc au terme d'un débat contradictoire, loyal, équitable insistent les textes internationaux, que les juges doivent décider de la culpabilité ou non de l'accusé, et en cas de culpabilité, de la peine la plus juste.

Toute l'architecture du procès pénal repose ainsi sur le principe du contradictoire, en droit national comme en droit international. Et le contradictoire, nous l'avons rappelé ci-dessus, c'est le rôle de la défense.

Nous avons, tous les avocats, souffert devant les premières juridictions internationales d'une regrettable absence de reconnaissance de la défense et de son rôle primordial.

Institutionnelle d'abord puisque nous n'existions que sous la tutelle du greffe, chargé de nous «gérer». Alors que le Procureur était un organe indépendant au sein du tribunal, disposant d'énormes moyens et de la considération de tous eu égard à sa mission de mettre fin à l'impunité. Peu se souciaient de savoir comment les accusés, déjà moralement condamnés de par leur seule situation d'accusés des pires crimes, seraient défendus.

En un mot comme en cent, la défense n'existait pas en tant qu'institution dans les premiers tribunaux. Et comme il n'y avait aucune autre institution susceptible de parler au nom de la défense, comme un barreau ou un bâtonnier, les avocats n'avaient la parole qu'à l'audience, pour la défense de leur client, jamais pour défendre la défense.

Or défendre la défense, c'est toujours protéger les droits des accusés à un procès équitable. Ce droit est un des droits de l'homme fondamentaux, un de ceux dont la Cour européenne rappelle qu'elle doit les protéger, non comme des droits théoriques ou illusoires, mais comme des droits concrets et effectifs [4].

Ainsi, défendre le droit d'un accusé, même accusé des pires crimes, à un procès équitable, c'est participer à l'œuvre de justice, une justice irréprochable qui seule, peut être source de paix et de réconciliation.

Un Bureau de la défense?

La création devant la Cour pénale internationale, d'un bureau de la défense indépendant fût à l'époque saluée comme une évolution institutionnelle salutaire, même si pour de curieuses et obscures raisons ce Bureau restait sous la tutelle du greffier, poursuivant ainsi la structuration instaurée depuis le début de ces juridictions.

Dirigé à la Cour pénale internationale par Maître Xavier Jean Keita, avocat, le Bureau du Conseil public pour la défense a au cours des années réussi à imposer son indépendance et à donner sa place à la défense dans l'institution, malgré les limites que lui imposait le fait de demeurer sous la tutelle et l'autorité administrative du greffe et de ne pas disposer d'une voix autonome.

Mais au moins s'agissait-il d'un progrès, d'une reconnaissance institutionnelle de la défense qui allait amener plus tard, devant le Tribunal spécial pour le Liban la création enfin, d'un Bureau de la défense comme quatrième pilier du tribunal, à équivalence avec le bureau du Procureur, la présidence et le greffe, chacun des responsables étant nommé par le Secrétaire général des Nations Unies. Même s'il s'agit d'un modèle encore imparfait, la défense

4. CEDH, 9 octobre 1979, *Airey c. Irlande.*

peut enfin faire entendre sa voix, dans et hors le Tribunal spécial pour le Liban sur toutes les questions qui concernent son exercice professionnel.

Le Bureau de la défense n'intervient pas directement dans la défense des accusés. Ce n'est pas, comme dans certains pays, aux Etats-Unis par exemple, un Bureau du *«Public Defender»*.

Le Bureau de la défense, au Tribunal spécial pour le Liban apporte aide et assistance aux avocats qu'il recrute puis qu'il nomme, les assignant ainsi à la défense d'un accusé, ou, en cas de procès par défaut, à la défense de ses droits et intérêts (article 22 du Statut).

Le Bureau de la défense apporte ainsi aux équipes de la défense (les avocats et leurs collaborateurs) une aide juridique, logistique et financière pour leur permettre de remplir leur mandat dans les meilleures conditions d'efficacité et de professionnalisme à égalité avec l'accusation. Il est en outre chargé de s'assurer de l'effectivité de la défense.

Le Bureau de la défense peut conclure des accords de coopération avec les Etats pour faciliter les enquêtes de la défense.

C'est ainsi qu'en juillet 2010, avant même le premier acte d'accusation, j'ai conclu un Protocole d'accord avec le Gouvernement libanais, représenté par son ministre de la Justice, afin de permettre aux futurs avocats devant le Tribunal, d'effectuer au Liban, leurs enquêtes à décharge.

En effet, dés lors que le Statut du Tribunal spécial pour le Liban n'a pas prévu de juge d'instruction, institution qui existe pourtant au Liban, il fallait absolument que les avocats qui allaient intervenir puissent effectuer eux-mêmes leurs propres enquêtes à décharge, faute de quoi ils ne rempliraient pas leur mission de défense. Il a fallu plusieurs mois de discussions, notamment avec les barreaux libanais, pour parvenir à une solution, autorisant les avocats, y compris libanais, intervenant devant le Tribunal spécial pour le Liban, à effectuer eux mêmes leurs enquêtes au Liban, malgré l'interdiction légale de rencontrer des témoins pesant sur les mêmes avocats libanais lorsqu'ils exercent dans le cadre national.

Ce Protocole a ensuite été très largement utilisé par les équipes de défense pour solliciter, comme il le prévoit, via le Bureau de la défense, la coopération de l'Etat libanais dans le cadre de leurs enquêtes.

Ce travail de reconnaissance de la voix de la défense j'ai tenu à le poursuivre auprès des plus hautes autorités.

J'ai sollicité et obtenu une audience avec le Secrétaire général des Nations Unies en mai 2014, faisant valoir qu'il avait reçu les présidents et Procureurs des Tribunaux pénaux internationaux mais jamais la défense. C'est ce qu'il m'a confirmé en début d'entretien en se félicitant de cette rencontre et me disant en substance « Maître vous avez la parole »...

Le communiqué de presse que le Secrétaire général a ensuite publié pour soutenir le rôle du Bureau de la défense, représente clairement un progrès majeur dans la perception du rôle de la défense.

J'ai poursuivi avec le Conseil de sécurité lors d'une réunion au Palais de la Paix à La Haye en août de la même année : j'ai dit aux membres du Conseil de sécurité, en présence de tous les présidents, procureurs et greffiers des juridictions internationales : « je suis sûr que c'est la première fois que vous entendez la voix de la défense ; tous les tribunaux jusqu'à présent marchaient sur trois pattes.

Nous sommes le premier Tribunal à marcher sur quatre pattes. C'est plus sûr ! »

Depuis 2013, profitant de ce statut d'organe indépendant, nous avons décidé de reproduire, mais au niveau de la défense, les rencontres qu'organisent régulièrement entre eux les Procureurs des Tribunaux pénaux internationaux.

Nous organisons donc des rencontres annuelles qui réunissent des professionnels de la défense, des professeurs qui nous suivent, des barreaux et des organisation d'avocats.

C'est ainsi qu'en 2013 nous avons été accueillis au Barreau de Paris, en 2014 au Palais de la Paix à La Haye, en 2015 au Barreau et à l'Université de Genève, en 2016 à *Middle Temple* et à la *Law Society* à Londres et en 2017 à Nuremberg, dans la Salle historique 600 du Tribunal, par l'Académie internationale des Principes de Nuremberg.

A Nuremberg nous avons présenté le résultat de deux années de travail par différents ateliers internationaux : un guide pratique des enquêtes pour les avocats, et un Code de déontologie commun dit Code de Nuremberg 2017.

Nous sommes fiers de ces réalisations que nous avons voulues pour qu'existe pleinement la défense devant les tribunaux pénaux internationaux. Non pour défendre des intérêts corporatistes, mais parce que nous croyons à l'importance d'une défense forte, compétente, effective et nous entendons donner tout son sens au mandat qui a été confié au premier Bureau de la défense comme organe indépendant.

Le chemin est loin d'être terminé toutefois. Il faudra encore bien des progrès pour que la défense soit concrètement et effectivement reconnue au même niveau que le Procureur, avec les mêmes moyens, financiers, matériels et humains, avec les mêmes droits, et les mêmes accès aux Etats.

La prochaine étape sera, nous l'espérons, la reconnaissance à la Cour pénale internationale, du Bureau du Conseil public de la défense, comme un organe de la Cour au même titre que le Bureau du Procureur. La reconnaissance, par les Etats et par la Cour pénale internationale de l'Association du barreau devant la CPI (ABCPI) est, souhaitons-le, un premier pas dans cette direction.

B. D'une monoculture hégémonique du droit à une approche multiculturelle : l'éloge de la diversité

> « C'est un grand agrément que la diversité.
> Nous sommes bien comme nous sommes
> Donnez le même esprit aux hommes,
> Vous ôtez tout le sel de la société.
> L'ennui naquit un jour de l'uniformité. »
>
> Antoine Houdar de la Motte (1672-1731).

Pour des raisons historiques, le droit utilisé jusqu'a présent devant les juridictions pénales internationales est essentiellement du droit de *common law*, fondé sur les principes et les concepts de la procédure dite accusatoire ou plutôt adversoriale. C'est en effet la puissante *American Bar Association* qui est à l'origine du règlement de procédure et de preuve du Tribunal pénal international pour l'ex-Yougoslavie (TPIY-ICTY) qui vient de fermer ses portes mais qui a inspiré tant d'autres règlements de procédure et de preuve, tant d'autres pratiques, et tant de jeunes juristes qui, souvent sans autre formation judicaire que celle-là ont ensuite voyagé devant nombre de juridictions postérieures armés de ce bagage, qu'ils ont reproduit comme seul modèle à suivre.

> « En effet, de nombreux juristes qui travaillent dans cette sphère internationale ne proviennent pas d'un système de la *common law* mais ont été *formés* à la mise en œuvre quasi systématique de la tradition accusatoire. Ainsi, d'anciens membres ayant travaillé au TPIY par le passé ont naturellement tendance à vouloir calquer le fonctionnement et les pratiques du tribunal à d'autres plus récentes. »[5]

5. Aurélie Aumaître, « La figure délaissée du Juge d'instruction en justice internationale pénale ».

Ce système n'a pas fait la preuve de son efficacité pour juger des affaires de crimes de masse. Encore ne faut-il pas confondre les principes de ce système, qui a incontestablement des mérites en droit national, notamment pour le respect des droits de l'accusé et le rôle plus dynamique des avocats, avec l'application qui en est faite devant les Tribunaux pénaux internationaux. Cette application est souvent très éloignée de la pratique élaborée devant les juridictions du Royaume-Uni.

Ce système a pour philosophie un combat judiciaire mené par deux parties, en principe égales, accusation et défense, devant un juge arbitre, qui ne connaît rien du dossier avant le début du procès, afin d'en avoir une approche parfaitement neutre.

Je vais parler maintenant de la pratique devant les tribunaux pénaux internationaux.

La procédure commence par une enquête menée pendant plusieurs années par un Bureau du Procureur tout puissant, assisté d'une armée d'enquêteurs et de juristes, disposant de moyens énormes.

Après la confirmation de l'acte d'accusation et avant l'ouverture du procès le Procureur est censé communiquer les éléments de son enquête à la défense *(disclosure)*, mais cette communication a toujours donné lieu à d'infinis contentieux tout au long du procès. D'une part parce que le Procureur décide lui-même des éléments qu'il communique en fonction de la stratégie qu'il a choisie «pour le besoin de sa cause», et d'autre part parce que le Procureur continue ses enquêtes tout au long du procès ce qui l'oblige en principe à d'autres communications, mais qu'il gère également selon sa propre stratégie.

> «En pratique, le Procureur choisit de produire le plus possible d'éléments de preuve, quitte à ensevelir la défense sous un flot incessant de pièces … La défense est alors obligée de faire preuve d'une adaptation qui force l'admiration, étant

> donné que la direction de l'enquête est souvent obscure ou du moins, dévoilée le plus tard possible. »[6]

Les juges n'étant qu'arbitres et se refusant à intervenir dans la stratégie des parties, n'interviennent qu'avec beaucoup de réticence et après de très longs débats, pour inviter le Procureur à une meilleure communication de ses pièces.

C'est au vu des éléments qui lui sont communiqués que, sur la base de l'acte d'accusation, la défense va elle-même conduire des enquêtes à décharge dont le but est essentiellement de jeter le doute sur la thèse du Procureur afin de tenter de démontrer lors du procès que celui ci a échoué à apporter la preuve qui lui incombe, de la culpabilité de l'accusé au-delà de tout doute raisonnable.

Telle est la pratique du procès adversorial international.

Celui-ci va ainsi se dérouler pendant plusieurs années lors de débats menés par les parties et non par les juges, débats en principe publics, mais trop souvent à huis clos pour des questions de sécurité des témoins. C'est d'abord le Procureur qui présente les éléments de sa preuve, et cela peut prendre des années, puis la défense. Cette présentation des preuves se fait essentiellement par des témoins, qui sont longuement interrogés par la partie qui les appelle, puis soumis à la critique de l'autre partie lors d'*examination* et *cross examination* dont se sont fait une spécialité les avocats de *common law*.

Cette pratique a incontestablement des vertus théoriques, la vérité étant censée «jaillir» du débat public contradictoire, de l'exercice *«examination- cross-examination»* auquel se livrent les parties, souvent avec une grande habileté, leur but étant, lors de ces joutes, de déstabiliser le témoin de l'autre partie, pour le décrédibiliser.

Devant les juridictions pénales internationales cette procédure accusatoire s'est révélée chronophage et budgétivore, malgré

6. Aurélie Aumaître, *op. cit.*

les efforts louables de quelques juges pour tenter d'améliorer les choses.

Les débats de procédure sont permanents tout au long du procès et parfois surréalistes comme si les parties ne maîtrisaient plus rien. Pour s'en convaincre il suffit de suivre quelques audiences sur ces discussions interminables au sujet de l'admissibilité ou de la fiabilité des preuves. A cet égard l'audience du 11 janvier 2018 devant le Tribunal spécial pour le Liban, dont le transcript est consultable sur le site du tribunal constitue un édifiant exemple et plonge dans un abîme de perplexité lorsque l'on sait qu'un tel débat se produit alors que le Procureur poursuit depuis quatre ans, presque jour pour jour, la présentation de sa preuve devant le Tribunal… dans un procès par défaut. C'est-à-dire un procès qui devra être repris à zéro si l'accusé est arrêté et demande un nouveau procès en sa présence.

Les *examination* et *cross examination* quant à elles peuvent prendre plusieurs jours, semaines, mois, voire des années dans des jeux de «pocker menteur» entre les parties, chacune ne communiquant à l'autre que le plus tard possible ses éléments de preuve, et chacune n'abordant que les faits qui «servent sa cause» de sorte que reste une zone grise, sans doute celle qui approche la vérité, qui n'est jamais abordée.

De plus, la longueur des débats représente un grave handicap pour le public, qui se lasse et ne peut plus suivre ces discussions totalement obscures pour lui et tellement loin de la réalité vécue sur le terrain par les communautés affectées par les crimes commis.

Contrairement au modèle de droit dit «continental» il doit être noté que l'accusation est représentée à l'audience par un avocat, qui ne parle pas au nom de l'ordre public – qu' en effet il ne représente pas – mais qui cherche avant tout à gagner sa cause comme évoqué ci-dessus, tout comme en face de lui l'avocat de la défense.

Le principe est bien celui d'un combat judiciaire entre deux parties, en théorie égales.

Ceci n'est certainement pas de nature à satisfaire l'objectif de recherche de la vérité assigné par la communauté internationale aux juridictions pénales internationales, pour les victimes et pour la réconciliation nationale.

La recherche de la vérité est précisément une autre différence majeure avec le droit continental. Cette différence est très bien expliquée par le juge Baudoin dans l'introduction au Traité de Pierre Béliveau et Jean Pradel. Je le cite :

> « On pourrait presque, dans un certain sens, caricaturer les deux régimes de la façon suivante : le critère d'excellence du système français reste la découverte de la vérité à travers une procédure inquisitoire, visant précisément à faire la lumière, toute la lumière, sur l'affaire et à permettre au magistrat de bien saisir l'individualité du délinquant ; le « bon » procès au Canada est, au contraire, celui au cours duquel les règles de preuve et de procédure ont été scrupuleusement respectées et donc où leur principal but, soit le respect des droits individuels de l'accusé, a été atteint. On pourrait presque affirmer que, dans un certain sens, la recherche de la vérité reste au second plan. La mesure du succès est donc très différente parce que les règles de procédure et de preuve n'ont aucune commune mesure. »[7]

Enfin une dernière différence majeure est dans la philosophie même du procès.

Dans le droit continental on juge un homme. C'est l'humain qui est au cœur des débats.

Dans le droit de la *common law* on juge des faits : l'Accusation a-t-elle rapporté la preuve, au-delà de tout doute raisonnable que X a commis les faits qui lui sont reprochés ?

7. Pierre Béliveau et Jean Pradel, *La justice pénale dans les droits canadien et français : Etude comparée d'un système accusatoire et d'un système inquisitoire*, 2e édition, Éditions Yvon Blais, 2007, préface, p. xiv.

Peu importe à ce stade qui est X ou Y. Quelles sont les preuves des faits ? Et comme on l'a dit des semaines et des mois, voire des années, vont être consacrés à des débats sur l'admissibilité des preuves produites puis sur leur fiabilité.

Pendant toute cette – longue – période, on ne parle pas de l'accusé. Et on n'entend pas sa voix. En effet s'il parle il doit prêter serment. (Cette règle a été un peu assouplie devant la Cour pénale internationale.) Beaucoup d'avocats devant les premiers tribunaux pénaux internationaux ont donc préféré ne pas faire témoigner leur client, de crainte du contre-interrogatoire que pourrait mener contre lui l'avocat du Procureur.

Dans ces premiers tribunaux il y avait ainsi deux grands « absents » du procès : l'accusé et les victimes.

L'accusé n'assistait à son procès que comme un spectateur muet. Le suicide en pleine audience, lors de la lecture de son jugement de condamnation, du dernier condamné du TPIY représente tragiquement le retour de l'humain dans son procès.

L'excellente recherche que mène le professeur Damien Scalia est très éclairante à ce sujet. Il a pu rencontrer plus de soixante personnes condamnées ou acquittées par le TPIY et le TPIR. A leur quasi-unanimité leur plus grand regret est de ne pas avoir eu la parole à leur procès, de ne pas avoir pu s'exprimer. Leur procès leur a échappé.

Paradoxalement l'expérience du procès par défaut devant le Tribunal spécial pour le Liban, si elle mérite de sérieuses améliorations dans sa pratique, s'avère plus cohérente dans une procédure adversoriale où le rôle de la défense, qui n'a aucun contact avec l'accusé et ne dispose d'aucune information de sa part, consiste principalement à tester la preuve – essentiellement technique – du Procureur, sans jamais porter la parole pour un accusé qui fait défaut.

Quant aux victimes elles n'intervenaient elles-mêmes que comme témoins pour l'accusation et devaient prêter serment comme tout témoin. Elles n'avaient pas de voix propre, autonome. Elles étaient instrumentalisées par le Procureur au service de sa cause…

Si leur situation s'est améliorée devant la Cour pénale internationale ou le Tribunal spécial pour le Liban, elles ne sont pas des parties au procès, contrairement aux procédures de droit continental, mais elles peuvent faire valoir «leurs vues et préoccupations». Leur intervention en tant que victimes et plus seulement témoins, dans le procès pénal international représente un progrès incontestable, mais leur maintien comme «sous-parties» dans une procès adversorial qui oppose deux parties, accusation et défense, n'est pas encore satisfaisant.

Comme j'ai eu l'occasion de le dire lors d'une séance plénière de l'Assemblée des Etats parties en 2013, ce ne sont pas les victimes qui posent problème devant les juridictions internationales, c'est la procédure de *common law* dans laquelle on les a mises, une procédure dont l'esprit adversorial, accusation contre défense, ne leur reconnaît pas leur juste place.

La procédure de droit continental, appelée inquisitoire du fait de la présence, à l'origine, d'un juge d'instruction (qui tend à disparaître dans plusieurs pays), est quant à elle, basée sur des principes très différents.

Les victimes tout d'abord, sont des parties civiles au procès. Si elles ne peuvent et ne doivent en aucun cas intervenir dans les discussions sur la peine à infliger à un accusé reconnu coupable, elles ont parfaitement le droit de demander au juge d'instruction ou au juge de l'enquête qui mène les investigations à charge et à décharge en amont du procès, des investigations qui leur sont propres. Ayant intérêt à ce que l'accusé soit reconnu coupable, puisque c'est la condition pour qu'elles soient indemnisées de leur préjudice, elles peuvent intervenir lors du procès dans le débat sur la culpabilité et même sur la qualification des faits.

Le dossier. C'est une autre grande différence. Dans le système continental le principe est qu'une instruction est menée en amont du procès, en principe de manière contradictoire, afin de constituer un dossier tendant à la recherche de la vérité, dossier contenant des éléments matériels rassemblés par des officiers de police assermentés ainsi que par des experts, légistes, balistiques etc., eux aussi sous serment, ainsi que des procès-verbaux de déclarations de témoins établis également par des officiers assermentés. Et bien sûr également les procès verbaux d'interrogatoires de l'accusé, des victimes et des témoins, établis par le juge d'instruction. Ainsi que, très souvent, le procès-verbal d'une reconstitution du crime ainsi que d'une ou des confrontations de l'accusé avec les victimes et les témoins.

Le principe de cette instruction est d'être menée à charge et à décharge. Même si dans la pratique les avocats se plaignent souvent d'une instruction orientée à charge, en raison notamment d'une trop grande proximité entre le juge d'instruction et le Procureur, il est notable que l'instauration d'un juge d'instruction avait pour but de procurer à l'accusé un juge indépendant, payé par l'Etat pour constituer un dossier impartial, tant à charge qu'à décharge. A cet égard la décision rendue par les juges d'instructions parisiens dans l'affaire de la rue Copernic est très éclairante, bien qu'hélas trop isolée, sur le pouvoir – pas toujours utilisé – des juges d'instruction.

A rapprocher des pays de *common law* où, si l'accusé n'a pas les moyens de s'offrir les services d'un avocat pour effectuer des enquêtes à décharge, il sera sans défense véritable face au Procureur. C'est ainsi que selon une étude de l'Université Colombia à New York, 90 % des accusés aux Etats-Unis plaident coupables, non pas qu'ils le soient forcément, mais parce qu'il n'ont souvent pas les moyens de se défendre.

Le dossier de cette instruction est ensuite transmis à la juridiction de jugement. Pour les affaires criminelles c'est le Président qui est responsable d'étudier le dossier à l'avance et de préparer minutieusement l'audience publique, qu'il dirigera sur la base du dossier d'instruction qui deviendra ainsi, public. Le Président établira un calendrier de la comparution des témoins et des experts, et déterminera à quelle date commencera le procès... et à quelle date il se terminera, situation aujourd'hui impensable en droit pénal international.

Quant à l'accusé: il est le centre du procès pénal. Quels que soient les égards qu'aura le Président envers les victimes parties civiles, l'accusé reste au cœur du procès.

Il est longuement interrogé par le Président, tant sur sa vie et sa personnalité, que sur les faits qui lui sont reprochés. Il peut s'expliquer autant qu'il le souhaite et ses propos n'engagent pas les juges, qui sont libres de les croire ou non. L'on dit ainsi que l'accusé à «le droit de mentir», mais que les juges seront libres d'en tirer les conséquences. Comme ils sont libres de tirer les conséquences de son silence s'il choisit de ne pas parler. Il peut réagir aux déclarations des témoins s'il le souhaite et être publiquement confronté avec eux.

Tout au long du procès l'accusé est donc partie prenante de son procès.

Le revers est qu'alors qu'au Royaume-Uni, dans la première phase du procès consacrée à la culpabilité et donc uniquement aux faits, l'on ne peut faire état du casier judiciaire de l'accusé, en Belgique ou en France, c'est au contraire un élément examiné contradictoirement, souvent dès le début du procès.

Le procès pénal en droit continental, romano-germanique, est donc d'abord le procès d'une personne.

Combien de fois ai-je dit aux juges en France: vous ne jugez pas seulement des faits, vous jugez un homme.

Permettez-moi une anecdote remontant à mes débuts dans la profession.

Comme beaucoup de jeunes avocats, j'étais commis d'office dans le cadre de ce que l'on appelle la garde pénale.

Un jour j'héritais ainsi d'un dossier particulièrement difficile. J'allais, comme de coutume, consulter le dossier au greffe avant le procès. Il s'agissait d'une affaire correctionnelle, c'est-à-dire pour des délits (vols, escroquerie) et non des crimes.

Après étude de ce dossier je restais consterné. Comment allais-je pouvoir le défendre. Tout accusait cet homme et en plus il était multi-récidiviste ! Que pourrais-je dire ?

Je me rendais alors à la prison, comme il se doit, pour préparer la défense avec le prévenu. Et là, je n'avais plus en face de moi un dossier, mais un homme. Un homme avec ses ombres et ses lumières, avec son histoire, avec sa famille, avec sa vie, avec ses grandeurs et ses faiblesses. Et cela changeait tout.

A cette époque je disais toujours au Procureur « Monsieur le Procureur, la défense sera toujours plus forte que vous ! Vous avez un dossier que vous connaissez très bien. Certes. Mais voyez-vous, le dossier je le connais certainement aussi bien que vous. Cependant il vous manque un élément majeur que vous ignorez et que la défense connaît, c'est l'accusé. L'accusé que j'ai visité tant de fois dans sa prison, dont j'ai rencontré la famille, les amis. De tout cela vous ne savez rien. Or ici nous ne jugeons pas seulement des faits, nous jugeons un homme ».

Je ne prétends nullement que l'un des systèmes est meilleur que l'autre.

Chacun à sa logique, sa philosophie, mais aussi sa pratique qui, comme on l'a dit, n'est pas toujours, tant s'en faut, à la hauteur des principes qu'il énonce. En ma qualité d'avocat français, j'ai suffisamment expérimenté les défauts de la pratique quotidienne de mon système pénal pour ne pas chercher à le promouvoir sans exiger de lui de profondes améliorations, notamment pour un meilleur respect du contradictoire.

On l'aura compris, le système de *common law* est avant tout un système qui s'attache aux faits, qui privilégie le combat judiciaire entre deux parties, en théorie égales, qui sera gagné par celle qui aura utilisé la meilleure stratégie pour convaincre le juge arbitre, mais qui peuvent aussi conclure des accords, notamment un plaidoyer de culpabilité.

Dans les deux cas il est considéré qu'il sera alors mis fin au trouble à l'ordre social, même si la vérité n'a pas été dite. C'est, pourrait-on dire, une conception libérale de la justice.

Le système romano-germanique, dit continental, s'attache avant tout à l'accusé et à la victime en tant que personnes, prises tant individuellement que dans leur contexte, et privilégie la recherche de la vérité, au moins judiciaire. De nombreux procès pénaux ont été menés dans des pays de droit continental, avec des centaines, voire des milliers de victimes parties civiles, que ce soit dans des crimes constituant des violations du droit humanitaires, ou suite à des catastrophes. En Amérique du Sud comme en Europe. Ce droit l'autorise et l'organise.

Pour cela il utilise le principe d'une instruction ou enquête à charge et à décharge, confiée à un juge indépendant payé par l'Etat pour essayer de découvrir la vérité. C'est peut-être une conception plus sociale de la justice.

Mais à ce stade convenons que l'on se trouve face un terrible malentendu : alors que la communauté internationale crée ces juridictions pour rendre justice aux victimes, leur dit-elle, pour leur permettre de connaître la vérité de ce qu'il s'est passé et favoriser la réconciliation, comment se fait-il que l'on ait mis en place dans ces juridictions le droit pénal de la *common law*, dont la philosophie est un duel entre deux parties, et où la recherche de la vérité n'intervient qu'en second plan.

Alors qu'elle est au cœur de la philosophie du système de droit continental, qui est cependant écarté.

Comment se fait-il que la *common law*, qui a d'incontestables vertus dans les affaires criminelles individuelles nationales ait ainsi réussi à s'imposer pour des crimes de masse devant les juridictions pénales internationales, sans s'interroger sur ce que pouvait apporter à cette justice cet autre grand système qui avait tant à offrir, notamment à travers la parole des victimes comme celle de l'accusé, le système de droit romano-germanique ?

En fait depuis le début des juridictions pénales internationales, les tenants de la *common law* ont imposé une monoculture hégémonique du droit, de leur droit, au détriment de la richesse que représente la diversité.

> «Lors de l'élaboration du Statut de Rome, il était pourtant annoncé le souhait de composer avec tous les systèmes, de produire une combinaison équilibrée. En réalité, le système accusatoire terrasse l'inquisitoire.»[8]

Certes il y a eu quelques résistances, quelques tentatives d'apporter un peu de cette diversité.

Ainsi selon Antonio Cassese[9], le fait pour les tribunaux pénaux internationaux d'avoir eu recours de manière fréquente à la jurisprudence de la Cour européenne des droits de l'homme a aussi permis de

> «modérer, si non de réfréner, la tendance de certains juges d'origine anglo-saxonne à puiser librement [dans] la jurisprudence nationale des pays de *common law* pour y trouver des solutions juridiques, en partant du principe que la procédure pénale internationale étant largement fondée sur le système accusatoire, il serait légitime de faire appel à des solutions

8. Aurélie Aumaître, *op. cit.*
9. A. Cassese, «L'influence de la CEDH sur l'activité des Tribunaux pénaux internationaux», dans *Crimes internationaux et juridictions internationales* (A. Cassese et M. Delmas-Marty), PUF, 2002, p. 143-182.

> élaborées par les juges de *common law*». L'utilisation des arrêts de la Cour de Strasbourg a constitué «une sorte de barrière juridique contre cette tendance».

Encore s'agit-il d'une vision plutôt optimiste puisqu'il est vrai que tant dans les procédures que dans le droit substantiel, les juristes de *common law* ont réussi à imposer leurs principes, leurs concepts... et leur langue. Or comme le disait le philosophe allemand Ludwig Wittgenstein, «les limites de mon monde sont les limites de ma langue».

C'est ainsi que les juristes arabophones, hispanophones, germanophones, francophones etc., sont face à un système discriminatoire à leur égard, qu'ils n'ont que le choix d'épouser ou d'abandonner, alors qu'en raison de leur propre formation, compétence, expérience, ils auraient tant à apporter à ces procédures internationales.

Quelques années plus tard le regretté président Cassese essayait encore d'introduire cette diversité et écrivait dans son Mémoire explicatif du règlement de procédure et de preuve du Tribunal spécial pour le Liban:

> «Par. 3. Pour réglementer la procédure pénale devant le Tribunal, deux modèles procéduraux doivent être pris en considération: le système libanais, de tradition civiliste, et le modèle adopté dans les tribunaux pénaux internationaux. Ces modèles ne sont pas inconciliables. Après tout, bien que fondée à l'origine presque exclusivement sur le système accusatoire, la procédure en vigueur au TPIY, au TPIR et au TSSL a intégré progressivement plusieurs éléments importants qui sont plus proches du modèle inquisitoire...
>
> Il s'agit là incontestablement d'une évolution positive car les spécificités et la vocation même de la justice pénale internationale appellent une approche plus inquisitoire (ou moins accusatoire): en effet, la poursuite judiciaire et la

> sanction de crimes internationaux ne mettent pas simplement en jeu deux parties adverses ; elles relèvent de l'intérêt général pour la justice et engagent la communauté internationale tout entière ... La nécessité de procédures pénales internationales moins longues, moins lourdes et moins coûteuses se fait indéniablement de plus en plus pressante. Enfin, le droit à un procès rapide fait partie intégrante des droits de l'homme fondamentaux. »[10]

C'est pourquoi je dis et je répète qu'aujourd'hui le droit pénal international n'existe pas... encore. Il n'existera que quand il intégrera, dans ses concepts comme dans ses procédures, la double culture juridique, *common law* et droit romano-germanique, ouvrant ainsi la porte à d'autres encore, provenant de sagesses africaines, arabes, indiennes, etc.

L'unité n'est pas l'uniformisation, mais l'harmonie des différences. La diversité n'est pas un handicap, mais une richesse.

Les juristes sont donc condamnés à faire preuve de créativité pour retenir, non pas le «meilleur» des deux systèmes, mais le meilleur dans chacun des deux systèmes, accusatoire et inquisitoire, et créer enfin un droit pénal vraiment international, ouvert au monde et à sa diversité.

C. Construire dès aujourd'hui le droit pénal international du XXIIe siècle

C'est à ce travail que s'attellent aujourd'hui des juristes des deux grandes cultures juridiques, praticiens de ces juridictions et qui en connaissent de l'intérieur les travers comme l'importance.

Nous proposons de construire dès aujourd'hui une procédure pénale internationale vraiment hybride. C'est le projet dit de

---

10. *Règlement de procédure et de preuve, Mémoire explicatif.* Consultable sur le site du Tribunal spécial pour le Liban : www.stl-tsl.org

« Solpérières » qui réunit des juristes, juges, Procureurs et avocats, de diverses cultures et nationalités. Ces professionnels du droit se sont réunis au sein des Groupes de travail dits « de La Haye » et de « l'Hôtel des Indes » pour proposer une procédure de procès internationaux tirant les leçons des pratiques actuelles et empruntant en effet à chacun des deux grands systèmes, leurs meilleures pratiques.

Ce modèle a été présenté lors de deux conférences, en 2016 au Palais de la Paix à La Haye, dans la grande salle de justice de la Cour internationale de Justice à l'invitation des ambassades de France et d'Espagne, et en 2017 au Tribunal Suprême à Madrid. Il fait encore l'objet de d'approfondissements. Il a pour ambition d'être finalisé à Rome en 2018, pour les vingt ans du Traité de Rome.

Le projet s'articule autour d'une procédure qui prévoit, après une période d'enquête préliminaire du Procureur d'une durée maximale de deux ans, de confier l'instruction de l'affaire à une commission d'instruction.

C'est l'innovation principale. Cette commission serait composée de trois magistrats : un ancien Procureur, un ancien avocat et un président ayant tous une grande expérience dans les affaires criminelles. Cette commission mènerait une enquête réellement à charge (sous la responsabilité du juge ancien Procureur) et à décharge (sous la responsabilité du juge ancien avocat) dans une perspective de recherche de la vérité. Des témoins pourraient être auditionnés contradictoirement à huis clos selon la pratique des interrogatoires et contre-interrogatoires, dans lesquels l'enjeu ne serait pas de gagner sa propre cause, mais de faire émerger la vérité. Les victimes seraient entendues par la commission, sans la pression d'un procès public et sans être l'enjeu de débats de procédure sans fin.

A l'issue de son travail la Commission proposerait un pré-rapport sur la base duquel les parties à la procédure (victimes, Procureur et défense) auraient six mois pour mener des enquêtes complémentaires si elles le souhaitent, enquêtes dont elles apporteraient les conclusions à la Commission d'instruction. Celle-ci, à la lumière de son instruction et des éléments complémentaires transmis par les parties, préparerait alors une ordonnance de renvoi sur le modèle de l'avis aux jurés que donne le juge anglais, c'est-à-dire après consultation contradictoire des parties à la procédure.

Ainsi serait transmis à la chambre de jugement un véritable dossier, commun à toutes les parties, circonscrit à l'essentiel. Le procès pourrait alors se dérouler en quelques mois seulement devant des juges qui décideraient du calendrier en concertation avec les parties, et qui mèneraient eux-mêmes les débats dans le seul intérêt de la recherche de la vérité, avec tout le respect dû aux droits de la défense. La procédure gagnerait en célérité et en lisibilité remédiant ainsi aux critiques qui sont trop souvent exprimées par les observateurs de la justice pénale internationale.

Telle est l'architecture générale du projet qui contient bien sûr des propositions de procédure plus technique qui n'ont pas leur place ici.

Sur le strict plan procédural, disons simplement ici qu'il nous paraît essentiel :

- de fixer des délais pour le prononcé de toute décision, de judiciariser les systèmes procéduraux actuellement en vigueur, de gagner en concision, de produire des observations et des mémoires revêtant véritablement le caractère de pièces de procédure et délaissant l'aspect universitaire qui les caractérise trop souvent (en particulier le recours excessif à des notes de bas de pages qui semblent parfois en dire plus que le corps même de l'argumentation),
- de veiller à ce que les juges, dont la professionnalisation serait accentuée, et leurs assistants, dont la formation judicaire serait également renforcée, remplissent pleinement, chacun à leur place,

leurs missions respectives, de donner aux victimes, généralement représentées, un statut de parties civiles.

Il est temps de conclure et de le faire sur une note positive.

Notre justice internationale pénale n'en est qu'à ses débuts.

Et pourtant. Qui aurait parié il y a vingt ans, qu'elle serait capable de mettre en accusation et d'arrêter le président Milosevic, le président Khieu Samphan, le président Gbabo, le président Taylor, et bien d'autres encore.

Certains qui ne sont pas encore jugés sont présumés innocents et feront valoir leurs droits devant la justice. Mais il doivent à tout le moins rendre des comptes.

Ils doivent avoir droit à un procès équitable, non pas un droit théorique et illusoire, mais un droit concret et effectif, comme ne cesse de le rappeler la Cour européenne des droits de l'homme.

C'est ainsi que la justice sera crédible, dans l'intérêt même des victimes, qui ont droit elles aussi à être présentes à leur procès, et à s'y exprimer en tant que telles.

Le temps où elles n'étaient que témoins au service de la cause du Procureur est terminé et il faut que les victimes aient toute leur place de parties civiles dans le procès international pénal.

Mais pour cela il faut absolument améliorer le système et l'enrichir de la diversité des cultures juridiques. D'abord les deux grandes cultures juridiques que sont la *common law* et le droit romano-germanique. Il faut concilier, ré-concilier ces deux systèmes qui ont beaucoup à s'apporter. Dans le même temps nous devons nous ouvrir à d'autres traditions, cultures, sagesses qui depuis des millénaires gèrent les conflits entre personnes et communautés et mettent en place des procédures de réparation et de réinsertion.

Le mot clé reste la richesse de la diversité et l'harmonie des différences.

En décembre 2014, avec un groupe d'amis, nous avons fait venir à La Haye, pour un concert au Palais de la Paix, dont le directeur,

Steven van Hoogstraten, était l'un des membres fondateurs du Comité d'initiative[11], l'orchestre pour la Paix. Cet orchestre fondé par le pianiste argentin et militant des droits de l'homme Miguel Angel Estrella, est aussi appelé l'orchestre des enfants d'Abraham, puisqu'il réunit des musiciens des trois grandes religions du livre. J'assistais à une répétition, avant le concert au Palais de la Paix.

Lors d'une pause un journaliste interrogeait le chef d'orchestre, Nader Abassi, égyptien, ancien directeur artistique de l'opéra du Caire. Il était entouré de deux musiciens, l'un venant d'Israël, l'autre d'Egypte. Le journaliste posait la question ; qu'elle est la plus-value de faire jouer ensemble des musiciens de pays, de cultures, de confessions différents ?

Le chef répondit : cela produit un son unique *(a unique sound)*.

Y a t-il plus belle définition de la diversité ? La diversité produit donc un son unique, irremplaçable.

C'est le vœu que je forme, en ce début d'année 2018, pour la justice pénale internationale.

Je crois fermement avec Gandhi, que la paix est le fruit de la justice. N'est-ce pas à ce travail de la paix par le droit que se consacre depuis des années, aussi discrètement qu'efficacement, celle qui est la mère de la justice internationale, la Cour internationale de Justice ? Combien de différents entre Etats ont été ainsi réglés par le droit.

Mettons donc en œuvre dès aujourd'hui, la justice pénale internationale qui sera celle du XXIIe siècle.

Une justice à laquelle adhéreront dès le XXIe siècle toutes les Nations membres des Nations Unies, en commençant par tous les membres permanents du Conseil de sécurité.

11. Le Comité d'initiative, qui est toujours actif pour d'autres manifestations culturelles et artistiques au service de la Paix est composé de Philipe Couvreur, Steven van Hoogstraten, Horacio Salvador, Frans Bouwen, Geert Corstens, Théo van Boven, Anneleen de Jong, mon épouse Evelyne et moi-même.

Une justice qui, par son professionnalisme, sa rigueur, son humanisme, puisant ses sources dans la richesse de la diversité des cultures et des Nations, sera préventive, dissuasive, punitive, réparatrice, réconciliatrice.

What Is There to Find for a Criminal Lawyer in the Peace Palace?

Alphons M. M. Orie*

It is a strange combination: Steven van Hoogstraten and myself in the Peace Palace. I have been working the whole of my career in the field of criminal law and procedure. Most of the readers of this book will know Steven as the General Director of the Carnegie Foundation. But Steven spent his last three years as a civil servant in the Government of the Netherlands in the Ministry of Justice. In that Ministry, which unfortunately was named the Ministry for Security and Justice from 2010 to 2017 and now, rightly so, bears its name in the appropriate order: Ministry for Justice and Security, Steven was deputy Director General for International Policy. As such he was involved in negotiating treaties and dealt with international drugs policy. Because my focus on international aspects of criminal law and procedure intensified, we could have run into each other already then. But I got to know Steven not in our professional environment. We share a passion for golf and both enjoy spending time in the Haute Savoie in France[1]. That is how we met and still meet. I imagined however how we could have met in the Peace Palace and what would have taken me there. What makes the Peace Palace an interesting place for criminal lawyers to go when they have not yet a friend there working as the Director General of the Carnegie Foundation.

Let me start with the a-typical circumstances in which I first entered the Peace Palace long before Steven van Hoogstraten took up office in the Carnegie Foundation.

---

* Judge in the International Criminal Tribunal for the former Yugoslavia from 2001 until end 2017. Member of the UN Mechanism for International Criminal Tribunals (MICT).

1. This has got nothing to do with the subject matter of the PCIJ case *Free zones of Upper Savoy and the District of Gex*, Judgment of 7 June 1932 (Series A/B, No. 46), though Geneva is our gateway to the area!

My recollection goes back to 1981. I had just joined the Bar at the Supreme Court of the Netherlands. That sounds very prestigious, but every lawyer registered within the geographical jurisidiction of the district court of The Hague was a member of the Bar at the Supreme Court of the Netherlands. They were exclusively qualified to appear in civil cases before the Supreme Court of the Netherlands. In criminal cases a defendant could be represented by any lawyer registered at whatever bar in the Netherlands. The system has changed in 2012 and presenting civil cases before the Supreme Court of the Netherlands is now reserved for lawyers who have passed a qualification test. However proud I may have felt with the prestige, for criminal defence lawyers it was just a title without any merits. But why did I go tot the Peace Palace as a junior partner in my law firm?

The domestic legislation for radio broadcasting was restrictive in the Netherlands and challenged by pirate broadcasters. They sought to escape the rather strict regime by unauthorized broadcasting from the High Seas. In August 1981 the vessel *Magda Maria*, flying the Panamian flag, had been arrested and seized by the office of the public prosecutor responsible for criminal offences committed on the North Sea. It was towed to the harbour of Amsterdam. It had broadcast only for a few days and had been monitored already for a long time by governmental intelligence agencies at the time it was technically equiped abroad for its mission. Even if the Netherlands could exercise its jurisdiction by prosecuting offences committed outside its territorial waters, the issue remained whether arrest and seizure on the High Seas was permitted under International Law. In my previous position at Leyden University my research had focused mainly on subjects of International Criminal Law but I failed to fully comprehend what made the Prosecutor believe that the arrest of this vessel on the High Seas was legally permissible. Representing the owner of the vessel I lodged a complaint at the

District Court of The Hague, claiming that the the vessel should be returned to its owner. The matter was not just routine for me and I therefore wanted to gain thorough knowledge of the Law of the Sea, more specifically about broadcasting from the High Seas and the extraterritorial exercise of coercive measures. It was one year before the UNCLOS was signed at Montego Bay. The new Convention contained detailed provisions in Articles 109 and 110 about the exercise of jurisdiction over ships engaged in unauthorized broadcasting from the High Seas It had not yet entered into force however. To have access to all legal sources, including foreign scholarly publications[2], the Library of the Peace Palace was a heavenly environment for me in those circumstances and also near to the premises of my law firm. By the way, it was not only heaven for me. I was struck by the fact that surprisingly often I had to place a hold on relevant books because they were on loan with another mysterious user of the Peace Palace Library. When the librarian finally pointed at the shadow user, I recognized him immediately: the President of the Chamber of the District Court who would hear the application! For those interested in the outcome: the District Court dismissed the complaint. The direct appeal to he Supreme Court however resulted in a decision in accordance with the state of the law in 1982[3]. The Library of the Peace Palce had not only allowed me to go deeply into this specific issue of Public International Law and the Law of the Sea. It also gave me a practical lesson in how to get to know your judge.

But let me get serious and focus on the question I put to myself: What would a criminal lawyer find in the Peace Palace?

2. I was especially impressed by Michael Haucke, *Piratensender auf See* (Pirate Broadcasting at Sea), 1969, which I read as if it were a thriller and which I never would have found in a local legal library.
3. See for this case H. Meijers and R. C. R. Siekmann, "The 'Magda Maria' and Customary Law at Sea – a Case Note" [on the judgment of the District Court of The Hague of 27 November 1981], XIII, *NYIL*, 1982, pp. 143-156 and the Decision of the Supreme Court of the Netherlands of 24 January 1984, NJ, 1984, 538. For a photographic impression of the story, see https://www.flickr.com/photos/offshoreradio/sets/72157668301483036/.

Let me first consider the time the Peace Palace was housing the Permanent Court of International Justice. Going through the the case law of the PCIJ in its entirety I found one case only which directly dealt with a criminal case. In the *Lotus* case[4], the limits international law imposes on states when they establishing extraterritorial criminal jurisdiction was the central issue. The *S.S. Lotus*, flying the French flag had collided on the high seas with a coal transporting vessel, the *Boz-Kourt*, flying the Turkish flag. On board the *Boz-Kourt* eight persons died as a result. France claimed that the exercise of jurisdiction violated international law. The Court ruled that for the exercise of extraterritorial jurisdiction no permissive rule under international law is required. No rule of international law that would prohibit the adoption of the relevant principle of criminal jurisdiction did exist. The victims were of Turkish nationality and the behaviour of the 1st lieutenant of the *S.S. Lotus*, Mr. Demons, took effect on board a vessel flying the Turkish flag. Turkey therefore did not violate international law when it prosecuted Mr. Demons, after he had gone ashore, before a Turkish court for manslaughter. The *Lotus* case underlines the broad discretion states have in establishing and exercising criminal jurisdiction as an asset of state sovereignty. The case reflects the traditional concept of International Criminal Law. This concept covered mainly issues concerning the establishment and exercise of jurisdiction and mutual assistance in criminal matters.

But already in the era of the PCIJ thoughts were developing that anticipated more modern concepts of International Criminal Law. Those modern concepts pave the way for establishing criminal responsibility for crimes that are recognized as extremely serious in international law, often violating obligations *erga omnes*. Not only serious violations of international humanitarian law, but recently also the crime of aggression claims its place in the catalogue of

4. *S.S. "Lotus"*, Judgment of 7 September 1927 (Series A, No. 10).

international crimes. I will very briefly elaborate on some of these thoughts.

The sovereign right for a state to wage war had prevailed for a long period of time before WWI. Whether the reasons for waging war were right or wrong, it finally was the state itself that determined whether there were good reasons to go to war. It was a hot issue before the conclusion of the Treaty of Versailles whether Germany by waging the war had violated international law. Clear criteria were lacking to determine whether a war was a *bellum justum* under international law. B. M. Telders, a prominent Dutch international lawyer, was not the only one who saw little positive merit in the distinction between the *bellum justum* and *bellum iniustum* in international law[5]. For bringing the German Emperor to justice it was not only required that the initiation of the war be a prohibited act in which he took his part, but also that such act entailed individual criminal responsibility. The formulation of the anticipated charges in Article 227 of the Treaty of Versailles is ambiguous: *supreme offence against international morality and the sanctity of treaties*. An offence against morality is not yet a criminal offence. The Commission on the Responsibility of the Authors of the War and on Enforcement of Penalities struggled with the question whether the Emperor violated legal or moral obligations. The same vague orientation is reflected in the final sentence of Article 227: "In its decision the tribunal will be guided by the highest motives of international policy, with a view to vindicating the solemn obligations of international undertakings and the validity of international morality. It will be its duty to fix the punishment which it considers should be imposed."[6] In the interbellum the prohibition of an aggressive

5. B. M. Telders, *De juridieke waardering van den oorlog* (The Legal Appraisal of War), Inaugural lecture, Leyden University, 16 October 1931.
6. For those interested in what judgment might have been pronounced I can recommend the virtual reconstruction of the trial in *Het proces tegen Wilhelm II* (The Trial of Wilhelm II), Tielt 2016, edited by Hans Andriessen *et al.*; the case is dismissed in respect of the charge of waging an aggressive war for this act not being a crime at the time it was committed.

war and individual criminal responsibility were further debated but this debate provided no clear answers, especially not in relation to criminal liability.

In this same period not only criminal liability for international crimes, including aggression, is discussed but even criminal liability for states becomes an issue. Vespasian Pella, a Romanian penalist, promoted not only criminal responsibility but also criminal responsibility for states[7]. But enough about the development of what were just thoughts about criminal responsibility under international law but did not materialize before WWII broke out[8].

The landslide happened in Nuremberg (IMT) and Tokyo (IMTFE). These Tribunals changed the landscape of International Criminal Law completely. The disputes about individual criminal responsibility came to an end and the accused were charged with and convicted a.o. for crimes against peace. But this all happened far away from the Peace Palace. And there was more to follow. The adoption of the Nuremberg principles, the conclusion of the Genocide Convention, the adoption of the four Geneva Conventions and Protocols additional to these Conventions and the conclusion of the 1968 UN Convention on the non-applicability of statutory limitations to war crimes and crimes against humanity were all milestones in the development of international law with a clear link to criminal responsibility. But in the first decades after WWII it was relatively quiet in the Peace Palace. The silent evidence of Nuremberg was in a deep sleep in its basement. The archives of the IMT had been shipped to The Hague. By decision of the Nuremberg Tribunal the archives were entrusted to the International Court of Justice and arrived at the Peace Palace on 14 March 1950. Paper documents alone amount to 250,000 pages. Not all the archives are in the Peace Palace anymore. They were

7. V. Pella, *La criminalité collective des états et le droit pénal de l'avenir*, Bucharest 1925.
8. E.g. the Kellog-Briand Pact (1928) is not very clear on this matter.

de-acidified and part of the collection has meanwhile been moved out of the basement of the Peace Palace to a better location for storage, with the Dutch National Archive. The paper documents were already digitized, as will be the grammophone discs and films, the latter to be stored at the Netherlands Institute for Sound and Vision[9]. After digitization accessibility has been warranted in a few major cities in the world. Negotations for a final solution were ongoing until recently.

Were these first decades of occupancy of the Peace Palace by the ICJ still calm and quiet as far as international criminal law is concerned, this certainly changed at the end of the last century and the beginning of this century. More cases touching upon the administration of criminal justice released the *Lotus* case from its splendid isolation. Still the new cases often revolved around the same issue: in what respect does international law raise an obstacle to the exercise of domestic criminal jurisdiction. These cases cover various aspects of criminal and international law. The two cases between India and Pakistan show the various angles under which the cases are introduced. In the *Trial of Pakistani Prisoners of War (Pakistan* v. *India)* it is the exclusion of jurisdiction over genocide cases Pakistan claims against India, encouraging trials in Bangla Desh[10]. In the opposite direction, *Jadhav Case (India* v. *Pakistan)* India claims that Pakistan has violated the Vienna Convention on Consular Relations by not granting acces to an accused and seeks the death penalty resulting from the flawed procedure to be postponed. The main issue in the *S.S. Lotus* case had been whether international law limited the discretion of the Turkish legislator in adopting such principles of jurisdiction as it deemed fit. In the new cases the issue was more often focusing on the immunity international

9. A Brochure was published in 2017, *Nuremberg Trial Archives*, [prepared by the] International Court of Justice, custodian of the archives of the International Military Tribunal at Nuremberg.
10. The case was withdrawn by Pakistan.

law provides to states in their diplomatic relations [11]. The exercise of jurisdiction over high-ranking officials of a foreign state and immunity *ratione personae* before domestic courts is central in the most recent, still pending, case *Immunities and Criminal Proceedings (Equatorial Guinea* v. *France)*, as it is in some cases I will later refer to. The inviolability of the premises used by the applicant's mission in Paris also comes into play.

In general one can say that in the last decades issues of criminal law and procedure more often are the subject of or are related to cases before the ICJ. The obvious reason is the intensified attention the international community gives to international crimes. Many treaties were concluded aiming at combatting crime with an impact beyond national borders. This led to hightened activity of states in the prosecution of international crimes even if committed outside their territory. Further the establishment of international criminal courts and tribunals impacted on the development of international law and the cases before the ICJ.

The treaties mentioned are dealing with serious violations of human rights (e.g. genocide and torture) but also with crimes which otherwise impact on the international legal order (e.g. transnational organized crime). These treaties impose on states various obligations. These can consist of an obligation to adopt jurisdiction broader than the classical territorial jurisdiction, to prosecute persons that have committed the relevant crimes or to assist other state parties in prosecuting such crimes. Sometimes the choice is left to either extradite or prosecute, in accordance with the traditional adagium *aut dedere aut punire.* One can see states

11. In the case *Certain Criminal Proceedings in France (Republic of the Congo* v. *France)*, it seems that apart from claiming respect for the immunity a head of state enjoys, the card of the adoption of the universality principle for crimes against humanity by the French legislator is played by the applicant, similar to what France did in the *Lotus* case. It is the view of the applicant that the French unilateral attribution to itself of universal jurisdiction in criminal matters violates the principle of sovereign equality amomg member states of the United Nations: Application IV A, p. 7. The case was withdrawn by the Republic of Congo.

becoming more active, often driven by victims, in investigating and prosecuting perpetrators who committed their crimes away from the courts that are seised to try these cases. The cases of *Arrest Warrant of 11 April 2000 (Democratic Republic of the Congo* v. *Belgium), Certain Criminal Proceedings in France (Republic of the Congo* v. *France,* withdrawn), *Immunities and Criminal Proceedings (Equatorial Guinea* v. *France)* are clear examples. Similarly in the case *Certain Questions of Mutual Assistance in Criminal Matters (Djibouti* v. *France)* it is France which, for very understandable reasons, seeks the testimony from the President of Djibouti in a case before a French court. A French citizen was the victim of a crime committed in Djibouti. The infringements on Immunity France had committed, as claimed by Djibouti, seem not to impress the Court. The insistence of France to investigate the murder of the French citizen apparently triggered Djibouti to start its own proceedings, now requesting France to provide assistance under the Convention on Mutual Assistance in Criminal Matters between France and Djibouti. The clear reluctance of France to assist Djibouti in its proceedings results in the Court blaming France for not appropriately motivating its refusal to grant the letters rogatory requested. It is an interesting case with the two opposite issues are at stake, diplomatic immunity as an obstacle to proceedings on the one side and granting assistance to promote crimminal proceedings on the other, meet.

In its effect the case of *Questions relating to the Obligation to Prosecute or Extradite (Belgium* v. *Senegal)* better known as the *Habré* case is convincing for this new tendency that international law serves to promote rather than to frustrate criminal justice. Belgium had requested Senegal to extradite Habré, former President of Chad, who resided in Senegal. The Convention against Torture and Other Cruel, Inhuman or Degrading Treatment or Punishment provided that state parties establish universal jurisdiction for torture, which justified Belgium to initiate proceedings against

Habré. Senegal, bound to either prosecute or extradite in accordance with the Convention since it had become a party to the Convention, had repeatedly denied to extradite and invoked all kind of reasons, interpreted by many as signs of unwillingness, for not prosecuting Habré. The Court made clear that if Senegal would not grant extradition it was obliged under the Convention to prosecute. This paved the way to a trial, which ultimatley took place before the Extraordinary African Chambers, based on an agreement between Senegal and the African Union. The Statute of the the Extraordinary African Chambers provided that the Trial Chamber and the Appeals Chamber would be presided over by a non-Senegalese judge, appointed by the African Union. It took more than twenty years of persistence by the victims, assisted by the Judgment of the ICJ, to avoid impunity for Habré.

One can observe that the classical theme focusing on international law in an obstructive role to the exercise of jurisdiction, even over the most serious crimes, is complemented by a new role in which international law supports efforts to bring to justice their perpetrators. Barriers, though not yet all, tend to collapse.

The *Habré* case is also special because the trial ultimately was conducted before an internationalized court. This was not ordered by the ICJ but happened to be the most efficient and practical solution. It may have been inspired by the establishment of other international courts. The establishment of the International Criminal Tribunal for the Former Yugoslavia had been a first step in the the proces of creating International(ized) Criminal Courts and Tribunals. There were many to follow. Apart from these Extraordinary African Chambers I just mention a few others: the Rwanda Tribunal, the Special Court for Sierra Leone, the Extraordinary Chambers for the Courts of Cambodia and, of course, certainly most important, the International Criminal Court. The establishment of these courts also triggered a new element in the law on Immunity. The case *Arrest Warrant of 11 April 2000 (Democratic Republic of the Congo* v. *Belgium)*[12] clearly indicates that diplomatic immunity and immunity for heads of state applies before domestic courts of a foreign state but not in relation to "certain international criminal courts", whereby the ICTY, ICTR and ICC are specifically mentioned. The Court thereby confirms that an important obstacle to the determination of individual criminal responsibility for international crimes, often resulting in impunity, is ineffective before international criminal courts.

Establishing international criminal courts sometimes resolves domestic dilemmas. The African Union thus assisted in the establishment of the Extraordinary African Chambers and the EU seems to have played a similar role in the establishment of the Kosovo Specialist Chambers and Specialist Prosecutor's Office.

These international courts exclusively have jurisdiction to establish individual criminal responsibility, whereas the ICJ deals with state responsibility. The criminal courts can impose penalties, the ICJ has other sanctions. It can order, for example, that a state ceases its wrongful behaviour or impose an obligation to compensate. Although it has not happened yet frequently, the subject matter may be the same before the ICJ and the respective criminal courts. The most illustrative Judgments are those of *Application of the Convention on the Prevention and Punishment of the Crime of Genocide (Bosnia and Herzegovina* v. *Serbia and Montenegro)* of 26 February 2007 and *Application of the Convention on the Prevention and Punishment of the Crime of Genocide (Croatia* v. *Serbia)* of 3 February 2015. Many issues arise when considering the ICJ and the ICTY covering the same questions in a different legal context. I just mention a few without elaborating on them. For the respondent state to have committed a wrongful act, it had to be established whether the crimes were committed. In the Croatian case it was established

12. *Arrest Warrant of 11 April 2000* (Democratic Republic of the Congo v Belgium), par. 61.

that acts were committed which qualified as *actus reus* of genocide but not with genocidal intent. This excluded also any judgment in relation to many of the violations of obligations of the Genocide Convention. Where it cannot be established that genocide was committed no failure to prosecute can be established. In the Bosnia-Herzegovinian case it was established exclusively in relation to Srebrenica that genocide had been committed and some failures to prevent or to draw consequences of the commission of genocide were established.

Many more questions in this context arise. What are the standards of proof? For criminal proceedings the traditional standard of proof is *beyond reasonable doubt.* For claims against a state involving charges of exceptional gravity the evidence before the ICJ must be *fully conclusive.* What are the elements of the crimes? Whether in order to establish individual criminal responsibility or to establish that a state committed a wrongful act in the context of criminal behaviour, the criminal court and the ICJ have to establish the elements of the crime committed. This requires an interpretation of the relevant law and the establishment of the relevant facts. What would happen if the interpretation of the provisions of the relevant Convention or applicable customary law were interpreted differently by the International Criminal Court/ Tribunal and the ICJ? And what would happen if the ICJ would find that the acts of state officials and attributed to state organs in relation to the wrongful act were different from the acts and conduct of the accused as established by the criminal court? Even if the ICJ accepts in principle as highly persuasive relevant findings of fact made by an international tribunal and even if it will give due weight to specific findings, for example of genocidal intent, it will still establish the facts on its own authority. The basis for criminal proceedings is the Indictment brought against the accused, whereas the ICJ may have to deal with an applicant state which chooses an approach diverging from the Indictment. The ICJ has dealt with all these (and more issues) and overall there is no inconsistency yet between the outcome of the ICJ proceedings and the ICTY judgments in the genocide cases. It certainly was an advantage that the Genocide Convention, despite the complex evidentiary issues it may trigger when genocidal acts are commited in relative isolation by individuals, is at least clear in the definition of the elements of the crime. It is still to be seen whether future cases on aggression before the ICC and corresponding cases on the legality of use of force before the ICJ will find similar harmony as was found in the ICTY and ICJ genocide cases.

The risk of divergence on legal issues does not only arise between the ICJ and international criminal courts, but also among the international courts themselves. In many respects no common standard has been established. Whereas the ICTY was assumed to apply well-established customary international law as embedded in its Statute, the ICC is bound by the Rome Statute. Differences are already noticed in view of participation in the commission of crimes (the concept of joint criminal enterprise in the ICTY versus (co-)perpetratorship in the ICC) and the various forms of command or superior responsibility. The same applies for standards of procedure.

The ICJ and the international criminal courts will find each other more and more in the field in which they are both active. In many respects they have become complementary in the completion of a mission that they have in common. That mission can be described as making international law instrumental in holding states and individuals accountable for the most serious crimes rather than to shield perpetrators from prosecution. An end to impunity beomes a common goal. Consolidation of common standards of substantive law and law of procedure is desirable. That is why criminal lawyers should go to the Peace Palace and why those involved in the work of the primary judicial organ of the United Nations should feel welcome in the international criminal courts. With full respect for their different tasks they should endeavour to avoid unnecessary clashes that would do harm to what should unite them: to contribute with their own means to justice being brought to numerous victims of the most horrendous international crimes. A thorough mutual understanding of the work of these courts is essential.

Having concluded that there is something to be found for criminal lawyers in the Peace Palace (and for public international lawyers in the premises of international criminal courts), I now return to my own personal experiences in the Peace Palace, not the library any more but some other room which I would be unable to find again. I had taken up residence there at the time the *Tadić* defence team prepared for trial. Lead counsel Mischa Wladimiroff and myself, partners in the law firm Wladimiroff & Spong in The Hague, represented Duško Tadić in the first case before the International Criminal Tribunal for the Former Yugoslavia. Concern had been expressed as to whether we would be able to cope with the common law oriented procedure before the ICTY. Our origin was the civil law oriented system of criminal procedure of the Netherlands. A special training in trial techniques by experienced US and UK defence lawyers was offered to us and that is why I resided for a week in the Peace Palace. Because Mischa Wladimiroff was suffering from a herniated disc and was bedridden, the training sessions were videorecorded from the room in the premises of the Peace Palace where the training was held. Being grilled for five consecutive full days on trial techniques by my teachers came down to pure torture. The fact that Mischa watched the video recordings in the evenings did not make this violation of my human rights any less serious and underlined my solitary confinement. It is the first time that I reveal this evil practice which took place within the perimeters of the Peace Palace. But my gratitude towards the Carnegie Foundation for providing inspiring training grounds – I still do not know why they were so generous – still stands. By granting hospitality to trainers and trainee(s) the Peace Palace certainly contributed considerably to my survival in the ICTY, initially as defence counsel, but certainly later also as Presiding Judge. When defence counsel from a civil law background (or even worse when they were common law seasoned practioners) were struggling (or playing) with the difference between leading and non-leading questions or the scope of examination in chief or in cross-examination, the lessons from my private education in the Peace Palace came to my rescue.

Since there are good reasons for criminal lawyers to go to the Peace Palace I finally wish to give them some guidance how to get there. The formal address may be at the Carnegieplein 2 in The Hague, but especially criminal lawyers may prefer to approach the Peace Palace from the adjacent footpath. This footpath was in 2017 named after one of the icons of international criminal justice and lead prosecutor of the Einsatzgruppen trial in Nuremberg: just follow the *Benjamin Ferenczpad*!

The PCA, The Hague Courts and the *Yukos* Case

Serge Vlaar*

A. Introduction

For some years now the European Union promoted the reform of and good governance in judicial systems in Central Asia. Part of this Rule of Law Initiative is the Rule of Law Platform – Central Asia. This Platform aims to support the objectives of the Rule of Law Initiative and has organized various seminars in Central Asia. On 19 May 2017 the Rule of Law Platform – Central Asia organized a seminar on States and International Arbitration in Tashkent, Uzbekistan. The participants were, on the one hand, students and legal practitioners and on the other hand high officials, judges and several politicians. The level of knowledge of the attendees was therefore rather varied.

The main topic dealt with during the seminar was whether, against the background of an investment treaty between the EU and the Central Asian States, dispute resolution by means of arbitration would be a good instrument. And, if so, what kind of arbitration proceedings would have to be chosen: should the parties to this new treaty opt for the classic BIT arbitration proceedings or would some kind of CETA proceedings be preferable?

I was asked to hold a presentation on the way the Permanent Court of Arbitration ("PCA") deals with investment arbitrations, what the advantages and disadvantages of these proceedings are and discuss the recent *Yukos* case[1], which has grabbed the

---

* Read Law and Philosophy at Groningen University and has been an Advocate in commercial practice for 35 years.

1. District Court, The Hague, 20 April 2016, ECLI: NL:RBDHA: 2016: 4229, setting aside three PCA awards of 18 July 2014, all three against the Russian Federation (see PCA website).

headlines a few years ago. The following text is an elaboration of the presentation I gave in Tashkent.

B. Background of the Permanent Court of Arbitration ("PCA")

In 1899 the first Hague Peace Conference adopted the Hague Convention for the Pacific Settlement of International Disputes (hereinafter: the Convention). Its object was:

> "seeking the most objective means of ensuring to all peoples the benefits of a real and lasting peace, and above all, of limiting the progressive development of existing armaments".

Article 20 of the Convention runs:

> "(w)ith the object of facilitating an immediate recourse to arbitration for international differences, which it has not been possible to settle by diplomacy, the signatory Powers undertake to organize a Permanent Court of Arbitration, accessible at all times . . .".

The Convention was altered in 1907, but, as far as the present subject is concerned, not in a material way.

These august words make clear that for the parties to the Convention peace was not so much an end as it was a means. The main reason for drawing up the Convention was that the most industrialized countries of the world were engaged in a financially crippling arms race. The main actors were Great Britain and Germany, followed at some distance by France. Out of sight from most Europeans the United States was also becoming a major industrial power, that would be able to enter the arms race at any moment it chose to do so. For many other countries participation in this arms race was financially and economically simply not possible. These countries, led by the Russian Czar, tried to promote alternative ways to settle differences. In this way, gunboat diplomacy could be replaced by discussions at the arbitration table.

At the time, arbitration was preferred to a national court. Having sovereign states accept a court decision from another sovereign state was deemed too difficult. If states would have a larger say in the appointment of arbitrators and the way that proceedings were to be held, it was reasonably expected that the award would also be accepted more easily.

Until the 1920s, when the Permanent Court of International Justice came into being, the PCA was quite active. Although only interstate arbitrations were heard, the PCA clearly saw to an existing need. The kind of disputes before the PCA were, for instance, boundary questions, mining rights and fishing rights. Since the 1920s, the PCA slowly went into a kind of hibernation, although it should be noted that since the 1930s arbitrations between individuals and states became possible. The cold war that emerged after WWII resulted in a climate that made arbitration difficult. The mutual distrust was simply too large. But since the end of the previous century the caseload of the PCA has grown considerably. The major part of that caseload consists of investor-state arbitrations.

In 2015 the PCA docket consisted of 100 registered cases, of which 58 were investor-state arbitrations. In 2016, 86 of the 148 administered cases were investor-state arbitrations under bilateral/ multilateral investment treaties or national investment laws, resulting in the same proportion as in 2015. These cases appear to have been the kiss of life for the PCA. It is nowadays quite an active organization. The only kind of cases it does not take on are purely commercial cases between private parties.

The PCA sits in the Peace Palace in The Hague, which it shares with, amongst others, the International Court of Justice. It is at the heart of a bustling international law community in The Hague, also consisting of The Hague Academy for International Law, which is lodged in an annex of the Peace Palace. This Academy is increasingly focusing its attention upon arbitration. One of the latest additions to the international law community in The Hague is The Hague Institute for Internationalization of Law, concentrating on the quality of justice systems.

The PCA is not so much a court as a registry, supplemented with a large list of names of arbitrators. Each party to the Convention can select four persons of "known competency in questions of international law, of the highest moral reputation and disposed to accept the duties of arbitrator" as members of the court for a renewable six-year term. The PCA administers cases, but does not adjudicate them as such. In cases where that is provided for, the Secretary-General of the PCA may appoint arbitrators (or appoint a body that appoints the arbitrators) and may hear challenges against an appointed arbitrator, but that is as far as it goes.

About 120 states are party to the Convention. Recently, Kosovo and the Palestinian Authority became party after fierce diplomatic fights over their eligibility[2].

It should be borne in mind that the PCA is in competition with various other arbitration institutes that offer services for investor-state arbitrations. For instance the International Centre for Settlement of Investment Disputes (ICSID) of the World Bank in Washington, the International Chamber of Commerce (ICC) in Paris and the Chamber of Commerce in Stockholm. All these institutes have their pros and cons. ICSID is often seen as an instrument of "the West" (generally not true), while the ICC is sometimes considered to be too much pro-business (probably not true). The PCA has its own position in this competitive arrangement. It is considered to be slightly more objective and, in

2. Kosovo is party to the 1907 Convention since 5 January 2016 and Palestine since 29 December 2015 (source: PCA website).

view of its long history, well-established. Its location in the world famous Peace Palace is also an attractive feature for all parties involved.

C. Investor-State Arbitrations

An investor-state arbitration can reach the PCA in various ways. Parties can agree to bring the matter before the PCA on an *ad hoc* basis, either in advance or after a conflict has arisen. The choice for the PCA can also be prescribed by a treaty, either multilateral or bilateral. These Investment Treaties appear to be the most common cause for competence of the PCA. There are now about 3,000 Investment Treaties (mainly bilateral) in place. These treaties all stipulate that any conflict will not or not necessarily be resolved by a national court of the state in which the investment is done, but rather by *ad hoc* arbitration tribunals. Many of these cases are administered by the PCA. Of course, parties can establish their own procedural rules, but most parties opting for PCA-administered dispute resolution services generally adopt either one of the PCA sets of procedural rules, such as a PCA arbitration rules (2012), or the rules adopted by the United Nations Commission on International Trade Law (UNCITRAL rules). The standard sets of rules can be adjusted if parties so desire. This implies that the procedural rules are generally rather flexible. I reiterate that the PCA is *not* the arbitral tribunal, but helps these *ad hoc* courts to functional tribunals.

The previous remarks concern procedural issues. But what about the substantive law, i.e. the rules defining whether the issues before the arbitrators are materially acceptable or not? Alas, the substantial law is not as advanced as the procedural law is. Again, parties can agree on a set of substantive rules, such as a national body of contract law, but will often take them "off the shelf" from existing sets of rules. Mostly these will be UNCITRAL rules, but if the applicable rules fail to answer the questions at hand, or if they are not applicable, arbitrators will ultimately revert to the Vienna Convention on the Law of Treaties. Unfortunately, these sets of rules are seldom precise enough to answer the question at hand. They will almost always require a vast amount of interpretation.

And here another trait of arbitration kicks in. Arbitrators are not bound by previous decisions of other arbitral tribunals. There is no such thing as *stare decisis* in arbitration. Of course, many arbitrators will tend to look at earlier decisions by other arbitrators and try to compose a body of case law. Unfortunately, this attitude is primarily found in arbitrators with a judicial or university background. Arbitrators from private practice tend to address matters more on an *ad hoc* basis. As James Crawford, Professor of Public International Law at Cambridge, put it at a seminar in December 2012:

> "There was a time that I hoped that normal deference to the opinions of others, and good sense and reference to authority might lead to gradual improvement. But there is a tendency among arbitrators to say 'we are the ones mandated to decide this case, there is no jurisprudence constante, and we simply decide it the way we think'."

It should be borne in mind that the quality of the arbitration depends on the quality of the arbitrators, their independence and impartiality. This is even more important in investor-state arbitrations, as the interests in those cases tend to be very high.

D. Criticism on the Current System of Investment-State Dispute Settlement (ISDS)

The present system of investment treaties, is coming under increasing public scrutiny. Many Bilateral Investment Treaties (BITs) were concluded in the sixties and seventies of the last century and are now expiring. The governments of states in which investments are done are increasingly not inclined to accept investor-state arbitration. South Africa is even univocally terminating its BITs. The public opinion is also turning against these arbitrations. I quote:

> "Remember that referendum about whether we should create a single market with the United States? . . . the government would not cede our sovereignty to some shadowy, undemocratic body without consulting us. Would it?
>
> . . .
>
> It would allow a secretive panel of corporate lawyers to overrule the will of parliament and destroy our legal protection. Yet the defenders of our sovereignty say nothing.
>
> The mechanism through which this is achieved is known as investor-state dispute settlement. It is already being used in many parts of the world to kill regulations protecting people and a living planet."[3]

And further:

> "If you wanted to convince the public that international trade agreements are a way to let multinational companies to get rich at the expense of ordinary people, this is what you should do: give foreign firms a special right to apply to a secretive tribunal of highly paid corporate lawyers for compensation whenever a government passes a law to, say, discourage smoking, protecting environment or prevent a nuclear catastrophe. Yet that is precisely what thousands of trade and investment treaties over the past half century have

3. "This Transatlantic Trade Deal is a full-frontal assault on democracy", George Monbiot, Opinion, *The Guardian*, 4 November 2013.

> done, through a process known as 'investor-state dispute settlement', or ISDS."[4]

Especially in cases concerning the environment, public health or human rights the public criticism of the present system of investor-state arbitrations has become fierce. Last year, a comprehensive Trade Treaty between the EU and Canada (CETA) nearly collapsed when the parliament of Wallonia, a part of Belgium, refused to give its consent to this treaty, amongst others because it contained a classic ISDS.

At the last moment this was solved by not only stipulating that only governments, and not parties, can appoint (panels of) judges for these arbitrations. This Court, when created, will be permanent and institutionalized. So it will not be, as in a classic ISDS, appointed on a case-by-case basis. In CETA, an appellate court is also provided. It was also agreed upon that the CJEU would be asked to rule, amongst others, whether this altered arbitration modus is compatible with European law. The Belgian government has entered a corresponding request into the docket of the CJEU on 6 September 2017.

The Transatlantic Trade and Investment Parnership (TTIP) originally also contained a classic investor-state arbitration modus. After fierce criticism the European Commission suggested to create an Investment Court similarly to the CETA court, which would be more transparent and would operate according to democratic principles. The basic idea would be that the arbitrators would be subject to strict independence and impartiality requirements and no longer be appointed exclusively by the parties involved. There would also be a provision for appeal. While welcoming this alteration, the critics still think it is not going far enough. They wish investor-state conflicts to be treated in the same way as any other

4. "The Arbitration Game", *The Economist*, 11 October 2014.

conflict by presenting the case to the competent national judiciary. Furthermore, the United States does not feel for altering the classic ISDS modus contained in the original draft. In business circles the alteration was not popular either. For the moment, this discussion is hypothetical, as the US President Donald Trump appears to be opposed to TTIP. The negotiations on TTIP have been suspended.

The EU-Vietnam Free Trade Agreement (EVFTA), for which the negotiations have not yet been finished, also envisages to provide for an investment court with judges who meet high standards of competence and independence, appointed in advance by governments and not on a case-by-case basis by parties. This treaty has not yet been signed or ratified, but the tendency to leave the classic ISDS is clear.

In view of the criticism against the present system of ISDS, the European Commission has decided that further action is necessary. It has recently requested the European Council for authorization to commence negotiations to establish a permanent Multilateral Investment Court (MIC). The idea is that this court would hear investment cases under existing and future trade agreements between (at least) the EU Member States and third countries. This new court could also replace the investment court system provided for by CETA and similar arrangements, if all parties to those treaties agree to this alteration.

It should be remembered that, whereas the EU has assumed exclusive competency for external trade policy in 2009, the CJEU has ruled in its opinion 2/15 of 16 May 2017 that a regime governing dispute settlement between investors and states falls within a competence shared between the EU and its Member States. As a result, each Member State has to consent if the EU wishes to include such a regime in a trade treaty. It should also be remembered that the European Commission is of the opinion that the ISDS arbitration modus of Investment Treaties concluded between Member States ("Intra-EU BITs") are incompatible with EU law. In a recent case, the CJEU had concurred with this opinion and has ruled that the ISDS arbitration modus of the 1991 Netherlands-Slovakia BIT was invalid because it may call upon a (arbitral) court installed by parties, and therefore not part of the judicial system of the EU to rule upon questions concerning EU law. According to the CJEU that would be incompatible with Articles 267 and 344 TFEU [5]. This decision has a consequence that the ISDS modus of nearly 200 pre-2009 Intra-EU BITs are invalid as well.

In its recommendation of 13 September 2017, the European Commission requested the European Council to authorize the opening of negotiations leading to a convention establishing a multilateral court for the settlement of investment disputes between investors and states. The aim would be: "having one multilateral institution to rule on investment disputes governed by all the bilateral agreements in place" rather than an investment court for each treaty. The Commission hopes and expects to meet the criticisms raised against the present arbitration system by:

> "setting up a framework for the resolution of international investment disputes that is permanent, independent and legitimate; predictable in delivering consistent case-law; allowing for an appeal of decisions; cost effective; transparent and efficient proceedings and allowing for third party interventions. The independence of the Court should be guaranteed through stringent requirement on ethics and impartiality, non-renewable appointments, fulltime employment of adjudicators and independent mechanisms for appointment."

5. Cf. CJEU, 6 March 2018, CLI: EU: C:2018:158.

I note that these requirements for adjudicators practically rules out the appointment of commercial lawyers.

If the Council follows the Commission's suggestions, the Commission will start discussions with third countries to get an outline for negotiations to set up a MIC. It is to be expected that these negotiations will take place within the framework of the UNCITRAL, which has identified the setting up of international investment courts as an "option for reform" of the present arbitration systems at the occasion of its 50th session in July 2017.

The system suggested by the European Commission would radically differ from the present arbitration systems. It will be largely similar to the system entered into CETA, but would cover all investor-state disputes. This would be achieved not only by stipulating jurisdiction of the MIC in all new treaties, but also by renegotiation of existing trade agreements concluded between the EU (or its Member States for pre-2009 agreements) and third countries. But the idea of a separate investment court, instead of the regular national judiciary, is still facing fierce opposition in some circles [6].

Is it all really that bad? Is the ISDS system fundamentally flawed? Should we seriously worry about the quality of work delivered by the PCA and other arbitration institutes and tribunals? As always, matters are a little bit more nuanced than they seem.

There is a clear trend in investment arbitration towards increasing transparency. Arbitration taking place in the full light of public scrutiny instead of in secretive back chambers is bound to be more objective. Nowadays, more and more PCA arbitrations can be followed live, for instance the Bilcon/Canada

6. See for instance "NGO's vinden dat de Europese Commissie vals speelt", ("NGOs feel that the European Commission is cheating"), *NRC Handelsblad*, 21 November 2017, p. E5.

(NAFTA) arbitration[7], in which the hearing was streamed live on the PCA website. New treaties also underline the necessity for full transparency. Not only are the UNCITRAL Transparency Rules often applicable, but documents are made available to the public and hearings are also open to the public. Interested parties, as well as non-disputing parties, can enter submissions. This transparency has made the whole process more accountable.

However, there is definitely a continuing problem. The counsel for parties are mostly recruited from the same small number of large litigation firms in the United States and a few barristers from London. Furthermore, there is a clear tendency in investor-state arbitrations to appoint lawyers from commercial practice (and mostly from the same circle as counsel) as arbitrators, instead of judges, legal scholars or diplomats (although judges are often chosen as presiding arbitrator). In combination with the fact that *stare decisis* rule does not apply, and the interests are often very high, this presents a large temptation for arbitrators to serve mainly the interest of the party that has nominated them. Of course, there is no clear proof that this happens, but rumours of this kind have been around for some time and the arbitration community has not been able to dispel them.

In the MIC proposal a solution was found by setting the standards for independence and competence of arbitrators very high and appointing them in advance instead of on a case-by-case basis. They will be mostly judges, and possibly academicians or diplomats. Whether this is a good solution is not clear. Of course, these judges, academicians or diplomats may be more impartial and independent than commercial lawyers, who are, almost by definition, partial, but commercial lawyers are also often more specialized and experts in the field that is being dealt with than judges are. A balance should be struck. A suggestion may be that in, for instance, the IBA

7. See site PCA (Case Repository).

rules of Ethics for International Arbitrators or the Guidelines or Conflicts of Interest in International Arbitration [8] it is inserted that if one has been an arbitrator in a certain court, neither one nor members of one's firm can act before the same court as counsel for a number of years and vice versa. In other words, one's firm either works as arbitrator or as counsel.

Whatever the solution may be, it is important to convince the public that arbitrators are indeed sufficiently independent and impartial to see that justice is done. This is a public relations challenge, but it should be undertaken, as transparency brings along public scrutiny and public criticism. And if the European Commission succeeds in making the initiative for a MIC a success, it can reasonably be expected that the present system for ISDS will only be applied in a diminishing number of cases. The docket of the PCA will shrink accordingly.

E. The Courts in The Hague

What is the role of the (Dutch) national judiciary in arbitration proceedings? Like most, if not all, modern legal systems the Dutch system has a kind of safety valve to ensure that completely unacceptable arbitral awards can be set aside by the judicial authorities of a country in which the award was made. Furthermore, in most, if not all, systems prior national permission must be obtained before an arbitral award can be executed in that country. In those proceedings the defendant can contest the granting of such permission. The defendant can also do so by lodging separate proceedings to ensure that such permission will not be granted.

The Dutch Code of Civil Procedure (DCCP) has a separate chapter on arbitration. Article 1058 DCCP prescribes that the final award in arbitration proceedings shall be "deposited with

8. See for both the International Bar Association site under "IBA guides, rules and other free materials".

the registry of the district court within whose district the place of arbitration is located". Article 1064 DCCP stipulates that:

> "Only the legal remedies of setting aside and revocation based on the provisions in this Section shall be open against a final or partial final arbitral award, insofar as the parties have so agreed."

The competent court is the court of appeal in whose judicial district the place of arbitration is located, the place of arbitration been determined by Article 1058 DCCP. Previously, this was the district court. In many PCA cases the place of arbitration will be The Hague. Therefore, the court of appeal in The Hague will often be competent to hear a case concerning the setting aside or revocation of an arbitral PCA award.

Revocation presumes actual bad faith, for instance presenting false documents. That does not interest us so much here. The setting aside of arbitral awards is a more relevant discussion. Requests for setting aside an award are far more common than requests for revocation.

The grounds for setting aside an award can be found in Article 1065, paragraph 1, DCCP:

> "(1) An award may only be set aside on one or more of the following grounds:
>
> *(a)* non-existence of a valid arbitration agreement;
>
> *(b)* the arbitral tribunal was composed in violation of the applicable rules;
>
> *(c)* the arbitral tribunal did not comply with its mandate;
>
> *(d)* the award was not signed or did not contain reasons in accordance with the provisions of Article 1057;
>
> *(e)* the award, or the manner in which it was made, violates public policy."

It should be noted that the request for setting aside an arbitral award cannot be seen as a provision comparable to appeal. The grounds for setting aside of an arbitral award are far more limited and are mostly applied under restraint. Exceptions to this restraint are the ground under *(a)* (the non-existence of a valid arbitration agreement)[9] and the fundamental right of the parties involved to present their arguments and express their views on the statements made by the opposing party *(audi at alteram partem)*[10], which falls under *(e)*. The Dutch courts will scrutinize matters concerning these two grounds in full. Whereas requests for setting aside arbitral awards are seldom successful, if they are it will mostly be after a request based on one of these two grounds.

The Dutch arrangement fits nicely into the international system. I refer to Article V of the New York Convention[11] which stipulates:

> "Article V
>
> 1. Recognition and enforcement of the award may be refused, at the request of the party against whom it is invoked, only if that party furnishes to the competent authority where the recognition and enforcement is sought, proof that:
>
> *(a)* The parties to the agreement referred to in article II were, under the law applicable to them, under some incapacity, or the said agreement is not valid under the law to which the parties have subjected it or, failing any indication thereon, under the law of the country where the award was made; or
>
> *(b)* The party against whom the award is invoked was not given proper notice of the appointment of the arbitrator or of the arbitration proceedings or was otherwise unable to present his case; or

9. Cf. Supreme Court, 26 September 2014, ECLI: NL:HR:2014:2837 (Ecuador/Chevron & Texaco).
10. Cf. Supreme Court, 25 May 2007, HJ 2007, 294 (Spaanderman/Anova) and Supreme Court, 24 April 2009, NJ 2010, 171 (IMS/Modsaf).
11. Convention on the Recognition and Enforcement of Foreign Arbitral Awards, signed in New York in 1958.

(c) The award deals with a difference not contemplated by or not falling within the terms of the submission to arbitration, or it contains decisions on matters beyond the scope of the submission to arbitration, provided that, if the decisions on matters submitted to arbitration can be separated from those not so submitted, that part of the award which contains decisions on matters submitted to arbitration may be recognized and enforced; or

(d) The composition of the arbitral authority or the arbitral procedure was not in accordance with the agreement of the parties, or, failing such agreement, was not in accordance with the law of the country where the arbitration took place; or

(e) The award has not yet become binding on the parties, or has been set aside or suspended by a competent authority of the country in which, or under the law of which, that award was made.

2. Recognition and enforcement of an arbitral award may also be refused if the competent authority in the country where recognition and enforcement is sought finds that:

(a) The subject matter of the difference is not capable of settlement by arbitration under the law of that country; or

(b) The recognition or enforcement of the award would be contrary to the public policy of that country."

The provisions of Article 1065, paragraph 1, DCCP can all be found in Article V of the New York Convention. For instance, the non-existence of a valid arbitration agreement (Article 1065, paragraph (1) *(a)*, DCCP) is a restatement of Article V (1) *(a)* of the New York Convention. The Public Policy referred to in Article 1065, paragraph (1) *(e)*, DCCP can be found in Article V (2) *(b)*.

This Article V rather limits the possibilities to refuse the execution of an arbitral award. As a result, it is often easier to execute an arbitral award in some countries than it is to execute a judgment of a foreign national court.

I note that the New York Convention states that recognition and enforcement may be refused. This implies that the standard provided for is a discretionary standard rather than a binding one. Courts increasingly refuse the recognition and enforcement of foreign arbitral awards. The courts of France, for instance, habitually disregard the setting aside by a court at the seat of arbitration and will judge autonomously whether the arbitral award is in accordance with its own, i.e. French, domestic laws.

F. The *Yukos* Case

A case that has grabbed the headlines in recent years is the *Yukos* arbitration. This concerns a set of three cases brought before the PCA by a number of western investors against the Russian Federation for the expropriation of the properties of the assets of Yukos oil company and eventually leading to its bankruptcy. I note that, apart from these arbitrations, numerous other arbitrations have been lodged between investors on the one hand and the Russian Federation or various Russian companies on the other, all pertaining to the treatment of Yukos. The ECHR has also been requested to rule on a related matter and found in favour of claimants that Article 1 of the first Protocol of the ECHR had been violated by the Russian Federation.

In the present cases, the Russian Federation contested the jurisdiction of the arbitral panel. This was overruled and claimants were awarded a compensation of about 50 billion dollars, with costs fixed at 60 million dollars for fees (i.e. about 75% of the costs made) and €8,440,000 for costs of the arbitration. The amounts already make this case staggering.

The case became even more staggering when the Russian Federation requested the District Court of The Hague to set aside the awards because the arbitral panel had not been competent to deal with the cases. The Russian Federation prevailed and the whole nine years of arbitral proceedings became null and void. Appeal has been lodged and further appeal to the Supreme Court of the Netherlands will almost certainly follow. But the question remains: how is it possible that arbitrators and judges have looked so differently upon a rather straightforward matter as jurisdiction?

Often questions that appear simple and straightforward are not simple once they are scrutiniously inspected. These cases are no different. The cases were brought before the PCA on the basis of the Energy Charter Treaty ("ECT"). The Russian Federation signed the ECT, but failed to ratify it. As long as it is not ratified and the state in question has not withdrawn its signature, that state will be bound provisionally. The Russian Federation has withdrawn its signature and has therewith terminated the provisional application of the ECT in 2009. The cases discussed here are based on actions of the Russian Federation during the period of provisional application of the ECT.

The main bone of contention was Article 45 of the ECT that provides for this provisional application of the Treaty (including arbitration)

> "to the extent that such provisional application is not inconsistent with its constitution, laws or regulations".

The question was whether provisional application of the ECT as such would have to be "not inconsistent with the constitution, laws or regulations of the Russian Federation" (which was the opinion of the arbitral tribunal) or whether (execution of) the arbitral award itself would have to be "not inconsistent with the constitution, laws and regulations of the Russian Federation". The District Court in

The Hague chose the latter approach and found that this threshold was not met. It all comes down to a question whether you stress: "such provisional application" (the "all or nothing" approach) or "to the extent that" (the piecemeal approach). As said before, the investors have lodged an appeal against the judgment of the District Court.

Probably, future treaties will be clearer on this point, but for these cases that was not relevant. Both points of view have their merits and I am not at all certain what the outcome in the end will be. What is clear, however, is that it is not so much the type of court that decides, but the fact that so many concepts in international law are imprecise and need extensive interpretation. But what is clear is that a court will consider its case law before deciding. Arbitrators have considerably more opportunity to apply their own interpretation and reach their own result. On the other hand, an arbitral forum is, as a result, more flexible. These are two sides of the same coin.

G. Conclusion

Investor-state arbitrations administered by the PCA are an efficient way to settle investment disputes. The proceedings are costly, but the interests at stake are often so large that these costs do not necessarily form an obstacle to use the PCA system. Two points that are deservedly receiving more attention of the public at large and the arbitration community are:

(1) the taking into account of previous arbitral awards and thus building up a corpus of case law;
(2) the independence and impartiality of arbitrators, which is sometimes perceived by the public as being inadequate, although exact figures are not available and the allegations have a large "hear say" aspect.

In a MIC system these problems will be addressed by having mainly judges as arbitrators. Probably this will lead to a more consistent case law and possibly to a larger measure of independence of the arbitrators, although the difference is mostly one of mindset, as judge-arbitrators often function with the same restraints (or lack of them) as other arbitrators. In this MIC solution, the attractiveness of a flexible, *ad hoc* system may suffer and judges are often not experts on the same level as specialized commercial lawyers. It is up to the policy makers which aspect they deem the most important.

The Universalization of Human Rights

Willem van Genugten *

Introduction

At the moment of its adoption, in 1948, the Universal Declaration of Human Rights (UDHR) was by and large seen as a self-evident framework for managing the relationship between states, individuals (and communities), a framework which still is highly relevant. The Declaration was also seen by the drafters as "universal", or better: as a set of "universal aspirations" ("a common standard of achievement") for all peoples and all nations, and for "every organ in society" (Preamble UDHR). This chapter does two things. In Part I, it tables three critical observations in relation to the often-heard categorical statement that human rights *are* universal. In Part II, it addresses the way forward, focusing rather on "processes of universalization" than on "universality" *per se*.

The chapter doesn't work with footnotes. However, all factual information or information referring to documents, can be traced back easily to reliable sources.

Part I: Three Observations on the Universality of Human Rights

1. The human rights framework is about more than the absence of torture

In the UDHR, the different human rights – civil and political, as well as economic, social and cultural rights – appear comfortably

* Professor emeritus of International Law at Tilburg University. Extraordinary Professor of International Law and, amongst other things, President of the Royal Netherlands Society of International Law. The chapter is partly based on and an update of a number of previous writings by the present author, a.o. his "The Universalisation of Human Rights: Reflections on Obstacles and the Way Forward", in: Sonja Zweegers and Afke de Groot (eds.), *Global Values in a Changing World*, Amsterdam, KIT Publishers, 2012, pp. 205-236.

together, from the right not be tortured to the freedom of expression, from the right to seek asylum to the right to adequate food. The latter is, together with other so-called "basic needs", expressed in Article 25 of the UDHR:

> "Everyone has the right to a standard of living adequate for the health and well-being of himself and his family, including food, clothing, housing and medical care and necessary social services, and the right to security in the event of unemployment, sickness, disability, widowhood, old age or other lack of livelihood in circumstances beyond his control."

I choose this particular article from the UDHR first of all because of its paramount importance, but also because in public statements NGOs and politicians often neglect that the human rights framework is about these "social aspects" as well. And there is more. According to Article 28 of the UDHR – another article from the UDHR regularly less well-known – "everyone has a right to the existence of a social and international order in which the rights and freedoms set forth in the Declaration can be fully realized". As do many other articles in the UDHR, this particular article clearly shows that human rights are not only concerned with the obligation of states to refrain from violations, but also with obligations to "provide support" (so-called "positive obligations") if people (and peoples) are not able to achieve human rights for themselves on their own strength.

Seventy years after the adoption of the UDHR, the human rights standards are worked out and further codified in a series of international and regional conventions and protocols thereto, and in a huge number of policy-oriented, quasi-legal texts, particularly those which are these days available to the UN Human Rights Council. Given the broad scope and high numbers of all these so-called "human rights instruments", it is clear that one must be cautious when assuming universality of *the* human rights. It would be impossible to claim that all these documents/instruments do indeed reflect universally accepted norms, let alone "always and everywhere". Each of the instruments and the particular provisions they contain would deserve close scrutiny, before that statement can be made, and before one can argue – based on criteria developed by especially the International Court of Justice, in a.o. and most prominently the *Fisheries* case (1951), the *Norwegian Loans* case (1957), the *North Sea Continental Shelf* cases (1969) and the *Nicaragua* case (1986) and in its Advisory Opinion on the *Legality of the Threat or Use of Nuclear Weapons* (1996) – that parts of them belong to customary international law, thus meeting the standards of *opinio juris* and state practice, or "even" to the domain of peremptory standards of international law *(jus cogens)*. The sentence "human rights *are* universal" therefore is a bit simplistic, and fails to fully recognize the importance of the is-ought divide (David Hume's "guillotine").

2. Universality is not uniformity: States have a margin of appreciation

The UDHR infers the notion of the universality of human rights in its name, thus referring to the (assumed) global coverage of its standards. See point 1. And while it is often said that the UDHR has reached the level of customary international law – which, again, remains to be seen, if one would take all articles, including their composing parts, literally – one has to take care, however, that in 1948 the United Nations comprised only 58 states, compared with 193 now. It was particularly during the 1950s and 1960s that many sovereign states were added to the list of UN member states, mainly as a result of the process of de-colonization, and subsequently through more incidental events such as the disintegration of states like the Soviet Union and Yugoslavia.

The question of what the 135 new states would have contributed to the discussions on the UDHR in 1946-1948 and what they would have done in a vote on this is obviously hard to answer with absolute certainty. However, for many of them it is well known that they subsequently supported the UDHR, be it in various ways, especially while meeting at the two World Conferences on Human Rights, in Tehran (1968) and in Vienna (1993) respectively. In the document of the latter conference, the UN member states endorse sentences in which the UDHR is again characterized as a "common standard of achievement" and "source of inspiration", even though it was also determined that the "significance of national and regional particularities and various historical, cultural and religious backgrounds must be borne in mind". The relevant paragraph from the standard setting Vienna Declaration and Programme of Action reads as follows:

> "We reaffirm that all human rights are universal, indivisible, interrelated, interdependent and mutually reinforcing and that all human rights must be treated in a fair and equal manner, on the same footing and with the same emphasis. While the significance of national and regional particularities and various historical, cultural and religious backgrounds must be borne in mind, all States, regardless of their political, economic and cultural systems, have the duty to promote and protect all human rights and fundamental freedoms."

On a positive note, the text quoted *(a)* repeats the indivisibility and interrelatedness of all human rights; *(b)* underlines the notion that they are mutually reinforcing each other; *(c)* restates the significance of national and regional particularities and various historical, cultural and religious backgrounds; and *(d)* emphasizes that all states have to live up to all human rights, "regardless of their political, economic and cultural systems".

But, on a more critical note, what about the interaction between these notions? What does it mean for daily international, inter-state practice that "the significance of national and regional particularities and various historical, cultural and religious backgrounds must be borne in mind" when states are discussing each other's human rights practices or when their own human rights practices are discussed by their peers? Many states are clearly willing to believe that the above quote can be seen as progress – which I do as well – also because words are markers of such progress and can be used in policy dialogues within and amongst states. However, one cannot easily hold that such a typical UN consensus formula adequately solves the problem of universality, not in the field of the norms, let alone in the field of practice.

Commenting upon similar words, used in successive UN documents, the Dutch Advisory Council on International Affairs, stated twenty years ago (1998), in an advice to the Dutch government, entitled Universality of Human Rights and Cultural Diversity, that "universality is not uniformity". This refers to the "margin of appreciation", which states do have with regard to the achievement of human rights. For instance, the right to fair trial is by many states recognized, but the paths to it may be very different. By way of extremes, one can observe states with a complete absence of an independent judiciary and states which actually have a very sophisticated legal system developed over many years. For both, the right to a fair trial is a "common standard of achievement", something they have to realize and live up to, but the roads leading to it are clearly different.

As to the "margin of appreciation" notion, it can be added more in general that some states are very young and have many other concerns, in addition to strictly human rights concerns, while again other states are trying to put an end to a left-wing or right-wing dictatorial past and cannot do so from one day to the next. Other states again have intrinsically political tensions that are at loggerheads with a number of fundamental ideas behind human rights. For example, in Islamic states, religion and state power are by their very nature extensions of each other. Nevertheless, these states are expected to commit to the freedom of religion, including the right to exchange one's religion for another one or for a non-religion, the core question being to my mind how tolerant they are towards other religions and to what extent they try to restrain their Muslim citizens from taking action against other (non-)believers. In such a case, the slogan that universality does not imply uniformity still applies, but also reaches its limits; it is no longer a matter of actively striving to achieve the higher goal (i.e. the full recognition of the freedom of religion), but of effectively removing the sharp edges of a government policy aimed at privileging a particular religion. This is as relevant in today's world as it has ever been.

So, while it would be great in the eyes of, especially, lawyers to separate discussions on human rights practices from all kinds of discussions on political, religious, economic issues, the reality is that they often *are* linked, desired and desirable or not. In an ideal world, discussions on human rights issues should maybe be above daily politics – more on that below, point 3 –, but the fact is that they are often part of it, and that it doesn't make sense to pretend otherwise. It would first and foremost lead to blueprints made at desks and disconnected to outdoor, hard realities.

That reality encapsulates the fact that states do a lot of window-dressing in the field of human rights, by inserting human rights standards in constitutions and by ratifying human rights conventions while adding numerous reservations and understandings, often on very a fundamental level and sometimes even against the "object and purpose" of the relevant conventions (which the

1969 Vienna Convention on the Law of Treaties orders to avoid). A case in point is the ratification of human rights conventions by Islamic states, which often insist that the conventions should not contravene Sharia law. One can think here of the position of women. Islamic states, for instance, have added interpretative declarations and reservations to their ratification of the Convention on the Elimination of Discrimination against Women. An example is the perceived incompatibility of the Sharia with Article 16 of CEDAW, which requires that states "take all appropriate measures to eliminate discrimination against women in all matters relating to marriage and family relations". The number of states that have entered reservations to Article 16, in whole or in part, is so high that the CEDAW Committee has voiced its serious concern on several occasions.

Other examples of links between human rights debates and political systems relate to communist-driven systems: think of weighing the (collective) general interest versus the rights of the individual. Further to all this, it should be kept in mind that sovereign states have central governments, the power of which is sometimes disputed if it comes to international legal obligations. One can think of a state like the United States and the question what governmental layer is responsible once it comes to, for instance, the obligation to provide consular assistance to foreigners kept in prison by one of the fifty states. See on that, the ICJ judgment in the *Avena* case (2004 and 2009), making clear that this is no doubt something which can't be "delegated away" to, in this case, the state of Texas, keeping Mexicans in prison, without notifying them of their rights.

Having said all this, it also is important to table *one overriding issue*: sovereign states are not (fully) sovereign anymore if it comes to their human rights practices. In the outcome document of the previously mentioned 1993 World Conference on Human Rights, it is stated that "the promotion and protection of all human rights is a legitimate concern of the international community". This quote basically says that states have the right to "mind the business of other states" once it comes to human rights practices. This might relate to all kinds of steps, from diplomatic *démarches* to targeted sanctions, and the like. The underlying idea is that sovereignty is not as absolute anymore as it has been in the past. The notion has been further clarified in a to my mind conceptually sound way in the context of the discussions on the "responsibility to protect populations from genocide, war crimes, ethnic cleansing and crimes against humanity", in short: the "responsibility to protect" (RtoP), a concept embraced by the UN General Assembly, during the UN Summit of 2005. This concept is often linked to the use of *military* means, authorized by the Security Council, in order to tackle gross violations of human rights, but in fact it is about much more. Given the focus of the present article it is interesting to refer explicitly to the report by the International Commission on Intervention and State Sovereignty (Ottawa, 2001) on RtoP that served as path breaking in relation to the concept. The report states, that, once a state become a member of the United Nations, "there is no transfer or dilution of State sovereignty. But there is a necessary re-characterisation involved: from sovereignty as control to sovereignty as responsibility in both internal functions and external duties". This is moving away from an exclusive focus on state sovereignty in a traditional sense ("mind your own business") to a focus where in the end human dignity is leading.

3. The (non-)willingness to accept external criticism

If a state becomes a party to a human rights treaty, that state is bound by treaty law (the state "consents to be bound by it"), including, in principle, the views and "General Comments" of the relevant supervisory committees. By becoming a party to a human rights treaty, that state basically agrees to accept the authority of the relevant supervisory bodies, allowing them to critically look at the periodic reports states parties have to provide. Further to this, and most importantly, the key question always is whether or not states have accepted individual complaint procedures, allowing as a rule people under their jurisdiction to address the international supervisory body once the national level doesn't satisfy them.

Apart from the above link between voluntarily ratifying treaties, there also is a series of human rights which have to be observed anyhow, whether states like it or not. These are the rights which Enlightenment philosophers such as John Locke would have described as (pre-state) "natural rights", and of which Jean-Jacques Rousseau would have said that people would have included them without hesitation in their "social contract". Examples of such rights would anno 2018 be the prohibition of torture and the freedom of expression and religion, but also, in the light of developments since 1948, the right to food or maybe even the right to (clean) water, being a right indispensable to the realization of many other rights, such as the right to life. In human rights doctrine and conventions, some human rights are qualified as "non-derogable", i.e., rights which may not be deviated from, even in times of emergency. Another label relates to the notion that some rights belong to the concern of all states, qualified by the International Court of Justice as "obligations *erga omnes*" (*Barcelona Traction* case, 1970). And again relevant is the question which rights qualify as *jus cogens* standards (see above). Linking that to international criminal law, one would also have to discuss the concept of "universal jurisdiction", which brings us back to the notion of universality of rights, basically meaning that these rights, at least a portion of them, transcend the political regulatory power of states. This is not the right place to elaborate on that, let alone to make a list of rights that for sure belong to the categories of "non-derogable", *"erga omnes"*, *"jus cogens"*, and/or "universal jurisdiction", alongside rights that for sure do *not*, and rights for which specific advocacy actions are undertaken and which might have already been "upgraded" by bodies of independent experts and/or courts, thus adding "legal authority" to work regularly undertaken by NGOs.

My view on all this is that it makes sense to state that some rights are more equal than others, that legal labels such as *"jus cogens"* are needed but in day-to-day inter-state practice are sometimes overestimated, and that it makes sense to take a very pragmatic starting point: *all* internationally recognized human rights are in principle universal rights, *unless* states can argue on good grounds that an exception to the rule is desirable or acceptable in their situation. A second aspect of that approach would be, that states should always be prepared to have their human rights practices discussed and assessed by relevant UN supervisory committees, and, if they are not a party to the specific UN conventions, should apply the findings of the committees analogously if it comes to issues that beyond any doubt belong to the categories of "non-derogable", *"erga omnes"*, and/or *"jus cogens"*. In addition, all UN member states already have to undergo periodical reviews of their human rights practices by the UN Human Rights Council, on all rights and whether they consent to that or not. This way, states which have negotiated an "elastic relationship" to certain human rights for themselves have ended up in a defensive position, being aware that in the last instance they are not the ones who can judge the legality nor the legitimacy of the room they internally created for themselves. Part of the problem is, of course, that many states are *not* willing to accept external control and/or the substance of that by bodies of independent experts or the Human Rights Council. If it comes to the treaty-based approach, it must be observed in addition that a significant number of UN member states did not ratify a range of key human rights conventions, while also many states do not have the political will nor the courage to become party to those (parts of the) conventions and/or protocols thereto that provide persons under their jurisdiction with the right to complain internationally about alleged human rights violations. By not doing that, they refuse to give individuals – and sometimes others – international *locus standi*, and thus more substance to the notion of external criticism.

Part II : The Way Forward

My point 3 above, is not only something which is in the air, and thus already forms part of "the way forward", but it also links to human rights violations that already take place. But how to avoid reaching that stage?

The UDHR formulated the destination seventy years ago, but left the reader with the core question of how to reach it, or to come as close as possible to it. One can easily observe that realizing a "life in human dignity for mankind as a whole" is a long, never-ending way to go. To mention a few present challenges: how about weighing the combination of poverty and climate change in human rights terms? How about measuring the effects of the use of technologically advanced weapons upon human rights? How about the human rights effects of civil wars? And on another level, in relation to "measuring" progress and non-progress: how about dealing with the fact that due to the Internet etc. we now know much more than we did seventy years ago?

The key issue of "the way forward" is without a doubt the "universalization" of human rights, thus strongly emphasizing the notion that reaching a sound human rights practice in each and every country first of all asks for a process-like approach, instead of (or alongside!) one in which states are told that human rights *are* universal and that they should act accordingly. The key words then are awareness-raising, empowering human rights actors, strengthening the independency of the judiciary, and progressive realization based on an interplay between political will and parliamentary as well as societal pressure, and all that depending on and in close relation to the specific characteristics of specific states. This is a bottom-up approach, with, in the end, the same sense of direction as the external, top-down approach: confront *all* actors in society with their human rights obligations and with their specific options to contribute to better outcomes. It might sound soft in the ears of some, especially those who believe that social behaviour can be changed by forceful means, but in the end there is no alternative to my mind. Of course, such action can sometimes be accompanied by political pressure, targeted economic sanctions and even military means, but in such cases the burden of proof of the effectiveness of the steps taken is in the hand of the action-taking state(s) and/or those who asked for such measures: do these actions indeed, apart maybe from short-term solutions for short-term problems, really contribute to sustainable human rights practices?

Having said that, the basic thing is to open up closed societies to new human rights inspired views. The freedom of expression, information and communication, the right to education, the right to political participation, and concepts such as tailor-made access to justice, may allow cultures to change in that direction from within. It should be recognized, however, that this is by and large a chicken-and-egg situation, in relation to which the previously discussed top-down approach can definitely play a role, as long as these actions are tailor-made, based on thorough knowledge of the power structures – central as well as local – and social characteristics of the relevant state and society concerned. Both approaches can help to break the vicious circle, in an interaction to be chosen from case to case.

In such lines of action, there is a huge role for governments as well as for the civil society (NGOs, local leaders, companies, churches, trade unions), in order to make the message – once again – tailor-made and thus more likely to be effective in the long run. And such civil society actions should not be conducted by representatives with legal training only, but also by people with a background in, for instance, anthropology, history, political science, theology and economics. This is vital to my mind, in order to make the discussions start from the right assumptions *and* to guarantee that the actions are contextualized as much as possible.

One of the key underlying problems to all that relates to situations of economic underdevelopment and the consequences thereof for human rights. On a normative level, it then helps to formulate (lack of) access to economic prosperity into human right terminology. "Prosperity" then might be defined as, for instance, the human right to adequate food and good health care, being central to the above-mentioned Article 25 of the UDHR. This is, what in many ways is done in the 2000 Millennium Development Goals and the 2015 Sustainable Development Goals. In fact, all (seventeen) SDGs contain human rights terminology, or identify approaches relevant to realize them. My personal favourites in the latter sense are SDG 9 (on a.o. inclusive and sustainable industrialization and fostering innovation), SDG 16 (on peace, justice and strong institutions) and SDG 17 (on global partnership for a.o. sustainable development). The latter can be linked to the above quoted Article 28 of the UDHR.

In practice, many developmental issues are seen as consequences of natural disasters and of climate circumstances and the like, in short: issues beyond the control of states' governments. However, in, for instance, the 2000 Millennium Declaration, accompanying the adoption of the MDGs, the UN member states' governments have made clear that they do see the issue of structural underdevelopment not only as something that "happens" and which is beyond their control, but also as a men-and-states-made phenomenon. Formulating the issue that way, it is clearly linked to the use of governmental political will and economic power, while the absence of progress in the field of poverty eradication and the capacity and preparedness to adopt adequate measures can be seen as the lack of using that power adequately or fierce-full enough, in order to, amongst many other things, realize education, housing, adequate health, a well-functioning judiciary for all. All this is basically about "human security", already expressed, be it in other words, in the 1948 UDHR and elaborated upon in concepts such as "sovereignty as responsibility" (see above).

To Conclude

Realizing human rights in full for all human beings worldwide, while taking the growth of the world population and many other present challenges into consideration, is sometimes coming close to the tasks given to the Greek King Sisyphus. There are indeed numerous actors and factors influencing and frustrating ongoing human rights concerns. Nevertheless, human rights have become a leading concept, gaining a lot of support and putting those who act against it in a defensive position.

As the UDHR states, nobody and no organ in society can look away if it comes to realizing human rights. This also goes for a range of governmental and non-governmental international organizations and institutions, based in The Hague, from the Hague Conference on Private International Law, the International Court of Justice, the International Criminal Court to the Mechanism that deals with the "left-overs" of the Yugoslav Tribunal; from Europol to the Office of High Commissioner on National Minorities of the OSCE; from large NGOs such as Oxfam to local courts and the ministry of foreign affairs, and from The Hague University of Applied Sciences to other knowledge institutes such as Clingendael, Leyden University, the Institute of Social Studies and the T.M.C. Asser Institute (and with apologies to all other organizations and institutes I could have mentioned as well). All of them have a role to play role on the long road, sketched seventy years ago in a document which is as relevant as ever before.

Global Protection of Human Rights. Who Can See the Wood for the Trees?

Nico Schrijver*

This contribution has been written in honour of Steven van Hoogstraten, former General Director of the Carnegie Foundation and the Peace Palace. For many years and in various capacities I had the pleasure of working with Steven on issues of peace and justice. He often engaged actively in debates on how to strengthen the rule of law in international affairs and how to improve institutionalized mechanisms towards this end, with particular attention to what the role of The Hague as the City of Peace and Justice could and should be. In great appreciation of his own contributions and his tireless efforts for global peace and justice, this chapter describes in a nutshell the development and codification of human rights at a global level. As part of that development, a multiple of international procedures to monitor and supervise compliance with the provisions of human rights treaties has arisen. Unfortunately, these monitoring procedures often work independently of each other. However, ideas to achieve an integrated international monitoring system within the framework of the United Nations, preferably with effective enforcement mechanisms, have, until now, not been warmly received by the international community.

A. The Universal Declaration of Human Rights as the Communal TV Aerial

As a response to the barbaric acts and disregard of human rights by Germany and Japan during the Second World War, the

* State Councillor, Council of State, the Netherlands, and Professor of Public International Law at Leiden University. From 2009 to 2016 he served as an independent expert of the UN treaty committee on economic, social and cultural rights. Currently, he is the president of the Institut de droit international, a member of the Permanent Court of Arbitration and of the Curatorium of The Hague Academy of International Law.

founders of the United Nations sought international recognition of general human rights that may not be violated by national states.

This aim had not been achieved in the Covenant of the League of Nations, the forerunner of the United Nations; for example, Japanese proposals for the recognition of racial equality foundered at the Versailles Peace Conference. The founders of the United Nations declared in 1945 that they were determined to reaffirm "faith in fundamental human rights" and they accepted as a purpose of the new world organization the need to achieve international cooperation "in promoting and encouraging respect for human rights and for fundamental freedoms for all without distinction as to race, sex, language or religion" (Art. 1, para. 3, UN Charter).

In order to achieve this goal, the General Assembly of the United Nations (UNGA) adopted the Universal Declaration of Human Rights on 10 December 1948. This Declaration, which was set up by the UN Commission on Human Rights, chaired by Eleanor Roosevelt and René Cassin, included civil rights and political freedoms of citizens as well as social rights.

The Declaration was solemnly formulated as a resolution of the UNGA and is hence not legally binding. However, the essence was quickly integrated for the most part in human rights conventions and moreover regarded as customary international law.

The provisions of the Universal Declaration are accepted everywhere today as the touchstone for the behaviour of states. Theo van Boven has colourfully described the declaration as the "communal TV aerial of humanity"[1].

1. On his life and work, see Fons Coomans *et al.* (ed.), *Rendering Justice to the Vulnerable: Liber Amicorum in Honour of Theo van Boven*, The Hague, Kluwer Law International, 2000.

B. The Development of International Human Rights Law

From the 1960s, a large number of human rights treaties based on the Universal Declaration came into being. In 1966 two fundamental covenants were agreed: the first on economic, social and cultural rights (ICESCR) and the second on civil and political rights (ICCPR). Both covenants came into effect after ratification by 35 states in 1976; the Netherlands did not accede to the covenants until 1978. After these two important human rights treaties, many others quickly followed. Often they elaborate upon the rights that are laid down in the Universal Declaration and the covenants of 1966. Sometimes they focus upon a specific subject, sometimes upon a specific group of people. Examples of the first are the International Convention on the Elimination of All Forms of Racial Discrimination (1965), the Convention against Torture and Other Cruel, Inhuman or Degrading Treatment or Punishment (1984) and the Convention for the Protection of All Persons from Enforced Disappearance (2006). Examples of treaties focusing on certain groups include the Convention on Elimination of All Forms of Discrimination against Women (1979), the Convention on the Rights of the Child (1989), the Convention for the Protection of the Rights of All Migrant Workers and Members of Their Families (1990) and the Convention on the Rights of Persons with Disabilities (2006)[2].

In 1993, at the World Conference on Human Rights the Vienna Declaration and Programme of Action was adopted in which it was declared that all human rights are universal, indivisible and interdependent[3]. This was consistent with the policy position of the

2. See Olivier de Schutter, *International Human Rights Law: Cases, Materials, Commentary*, Cambridge, CUP, 2nd ed., 2014.
3. See the Declaration and Action Programme of the World Conference on Human Rights in Vienna, in UN Doc. A/CONF. 157/23, 1993.

United Nations in discussions of this subject after the end of the Cold War.

C. International Monitoring and Supervisory Procedures

The monitoring of compliance with human rights treaties takes place at the global level principally in the supervisory committees that have been set up by the different human rights treaties. These treaty committees consist mostly of independent experts who are appointed for fixed terms. Their task consists of the following:

Reporting duty: States usually have the duty to report every five years on the efforts they have made to improve the human rights situation in their country, as laid down in the relevant treaty ("self-reporting"). On the basis of this report, the treaty body can ask questions of the state and make comments. Non-governmental organizations can also be consulted ("shadow reports"). Besides "naming and shaming", sanction options are minimal as the conclusions and recommendations of the treaty committee on the basis of the reports are not binding.

State complaint procedure: States can submit a complaint regarding the human rights situation in another state. The state complaint procedure is mostly only applicable if both the complainant state and the accused state have explicitly recognized the authority of the treaty body to deal with the complaint. This procedure is barely used due to the inherent political sensitivity. States usually choose for more diplomatic methods or for economic sanctions. Furthermore, human rights violations rarely affect the other treaty party directly which means there is less urgency and need to make use of this procedure.

Independent inquiry: In some cases, the treaty body can decide to institute an inquiry into the human rights situation in a state from the perspective of the provisions of the relevant treaty. This method occurs in only a limited number of treaties including the UN conventions against torture and for women's rights as well as within the framework of the Council of Europe (also in reference to torture). In the Anti-Torture Convention (Articles 20 and 28) a state can choose to opt out of granting this power to the committee. The UN women's rights treaty and the optional protocol to the ICESCR (in force since 2013) also allow an independent investigation by the relevant treaty committees. A treaty committee can usually institute an investigation if there are sufficient indications that there is a question of systematic and flagrant violation of human rights, for example, the practice of torture. The report, which is drawn up on the basis of such an investigation, is, in principle, not binding nor made public. This usually occurs in situations in which the state concerned does not respond, or not respond satisfactorily, to the investigation.

Individual complaint procedures: Some treaties allow an individual to submit a complaint against a state that violates his or her human rights. At the present time, this procedure applies to the European Convention for the Protection of Human Rights (ECPHR), the Convention Against Racial Discrimination, the ICCPR, the UN Convention Against Torture, The Convention Against the Discrimination of Women and also, since 2013, the Protocol to the ICESCR (which has still not been ratified by the Netherlands). The individual complaint procedure is optional in all these cases. Consequently, an individual can only submit a complaint if the national state has authorized the treaty committee to deal with complaints of subjects. Furthermore, there are, in general, conditions attached to individual complaint procedures. Firstly, the complainant himself or herself must be the victim of the violation. A complaint on behalf of another or in the general interest, the so-called *actio popularis*, will be declared inadmissible. Secondly, recourse to national law must be exhausted before the procedure is accepted by the committee. This means that there must be no single procedure still available at the national level to the complainant. Thirdly, there are usually time limits for the submission of a complaint and the response of the relevant body to the complaint. Fourthly, after the committee has declared the complaint admissible, it must first request a response from the state. This is followed by a procedure in which both sides present their cases. The UN committee then gives its "view" which is not a formal pronouncement in a dispute but a formulation of the findings of the relevant treaty committee. These procedures are hence referred to as quasi-judicial. Even when they formally have the status of a recommendation, these views are nevertheless usually described as an authoritative interpretation of the relevant treaty which is still adhered to by the national government. The procedures of the UN committees have clearly been inspired by the European Convention on Human Rights and Fundamental Freedoms that came into being in 1950.

D. Charter and Charter-based Organs for Human Rights Protection

In addition to the ten treaty committees, the High Commissioner for Human Rights, the UN General Assembly, the Human Rights Council and the Security Council also play a role in the monitoring of human rights treaties. Since 1993 a High Commissioner for Human Rights heads the UN Office for Human Rights ; the current incumbent is the former Jordanian UN Ambassador, Prince Zeid Ra'ad Al Hussein. Every autumn, the Third Committee (for Social, Humanitarian and Cultural Affairs) of the UNGA discusses the state of human rights in the world. This discussion focuses on both certain difficult human rights situations (in for example Cuba, Iran, Venezuela, the occupied Palestinian territories and Yemen) and on certain themes such as blasphemy, the rights of sexual minorities and the right to food.

In 2006, the UN Human Rights Council replaced the UN Commission on Human Rights as the specialized body to advise the UNGA due to continual criticism of the latter's double standards and politicization. In contradistinction to the now defunct Commission, the Council enjoys an improved organizational position as it falls directly under the UNGA. Furthermore, the longer duration and increased frequency of its sittings reflect the greater importance of human rights within the UN system[4]. Another innovation is the Universal Periodic Review (UPR), a sort of global human rights examination that all member states – whether or not they are parties to human rights treaties – must take once every four and a half years. This takes place, however, in the presence of their peers – not independent experts. Consequently, the UPR has a political character in contrast to the work of the treaty committees which are expected to consist of independent experts (although this is not always the case). Moreover, the UPR procedure is much more succinct with less documentation than is usual for the treaty committees. Furthermore, the UPR has virtually no formal complaint procedures available for individual citizens. Nevertheless, in the ten years of its existence, the UPR has developed into an important means of regularly assessing the adherence of each member state to global human rights standards and of asking pertinent questions about the domestic observance of human rights treaties[5]. This process makes use not only of the reports of the government concerned itself but also of information gained from UN institutions and non-governmental organizations.

4. See Nico Schrijver, "The UN Human Rights Council: A New 'Society of the Committed' or just Old Wine in New Bottles?", in *Leiden Journal of International Law*, Vol. 20 (2007), No. 4, pp. 809-823.
5. See Hilary Charlesworth and Emma Larkin (eds), *Human Rights and the Universal Periodic Review, Rituals and Ritualism*, Cambridge, Cambridge University Press, 2015.

A colourful collection of NGOs also attempts to attend the sittings of the Council in Geneva and lets its voice be heard through an array of various demonstrations. The sittings of the Council are hence becoming increasingly global rallies in favour of human rights.

Moreover, the Council for Human Rights can avail itself of a variety of so-called special procedures, in particular the appointment of independent country rapporteurs (currently totalling 14) and thematic rapporteurs (currently 41) who provide the Council with their reports of comprehensive information and recommendations on an annual basis.

Finally, the Security Council, particularly after the end of the Cold War, has started to give more attention to the connection between respect for human rights and peace and security. The Council now does this invariably as part of its country resolutions (for example, on Syria, Myanmar, Iran and Yemen) but also in thematic resolutions or declarations, for example, on the protection of citizens during armed conflict, the prosecution of war criminals, respect for human rights during UN peace operations and the responsibility to protect[6].

E. Conclusion and Possible Paths towards Reform

Anyone surveying all these developments will, on one hand, be impressed by the enormous efforts that have been made since 1945 to firmly establish respect for human rights and to advance a great number of international procedures to monitor these rights. No state today would any longer dare to claim that human rights are purely a domestic matter. On the other hand, as a result of

6. See the Advisory Council on International Affairs, *The Netherlands and the "Responsibility to Protect: The Responsibility to Protect People from Mass Atrocities"*, report No. 70, The Hague, 2010.

the proliferation of all these separate and specific procedures, it is often difficult to see the wood for the trees[7]. It is clear that we are very far removed from the ideal that was so alive shortly after the foundation of the United Nations, namely a Bill of Rights in the form of a trinity consisting of the Universal Declaration, one worldwide treaty and one monitoring committee. In practice, a maze of different and partly overlapping procedures has grown. Despite all the differences between, for example, the ten treaty committees, their mandates coincide to a degree, for instance for the right to equal treatment of men and women, the right to freedom of expression or the right to form a trade union. They also have similar complaint procedures[8]. Some small improvements have also been achieved when the treaty committees have been able to work together. The secretariats of all treaty committees, for example, operate under the aegis of the High Commissioner and they are housed in the same building (Palais Wilson, Geneva). Incoming complaints and petitions are first screened there by one common body – the joint petition unit. For several years now, all treaty committees allow the treaty states to submit a common basic report, called the common core document, on the human rights situation in their country to which they can then add per treaty a specific report on their compliance with the provisions on the rights contained in that treaty. In 2014, the committees on women's rights and children's rights also experimented with the publication of a joint General Comment on harmful practices of violations of the rights of women and girls including genital mutilation, child marriages and polygamy. However, the establishment of a single treaty body with joint complaint procedures lies very far in the

7. Surya Subedi, *The Effectiveness of the UN Human Rights System. Reform and the Judicialisation of Human Rights*, Oxon/New York, Routledge, 2017.
8. Wouter van den Hole, *The Procedures before the Human Rights Treaty Bodies. Divergence or Convergence*, Antwerp, Intersentia, 2004.

future[9]. Arguments in favour of streamlining the existing treaties and of eventually transforming them into one single global treaty have largely fallen on deaf man's ears[10]. Similar treatment can be expected for proposals to establish a World Court for Human Rights in place of the existing ten treaty committees[11]. In reality, the states parties are a long way from establishing such a World Court. It could even be counter-productive and undermine the universality of human rights as it is certain that a considerably smaller number of states would sign up to such a World Court than the 170 states which are now party to the ICCPR, the 167 to the ICESCR or the impressive 196 to the Children's Rights convention. It is even unlikely that the number of 123 member states that have joined the International Criminal Court would be repeated for a World Human Rights Court. The colourful, multi-track system of international monitoring by means of recommendations and a little "naming and shaming", which is embodied in the current treaty system, is simply not yet ready to be replaced by a World Court that has sole monitoring competence and can employ coercive measures. But these distant views are sometimes necessary to create a climate that enables an array of further small steps to facilitate better interaction and cooperation between the treaty committees themselves and between the treaty committees and the relevant UN political bodies such as the Third Committee of the UNGA, the UN Human Rights Council and the Security

9. On this issue, see the Advisory Council on International Affairs, *The UN Human Rights Treaty System: Strengthening the System Step by Step in a Politically Charged Context*, report No. 57, The Hague, 2007.

10. Nico Schrijver, "Paving the Way Towards . . . One World Wide Human Rights Treaty", in *Netherlands Human Rights Quarterly*, Vol. 29 (2011), No. 3, pp. 257-260.

11. See several contributions by Manfred Nowak, including "World Court of Human Rights. Utopia?", in I. Lintel, A. Buyse and B. Gonigle Leyh (eds.), *Defending Human Rights: Tools for Justice: Volume in Honour of Professor Fried van Hoof*, Cambridge, Intersentia, 2012, pp. 161-169; Jan Lhotsky, "The UN Mechanism for Human Rights Protection: Strengthening Treaty Bodies in Light of a Proposal to Create a World Court of Human Rights", in *Journal of Eurasian Law*, Year 9 (2016), No. 1, pp. 109-122.

Council[12]. If in 2018, the 70-year commemoration of the adoption of the Universal Declaration can be grasped to promote these steps, it would be a useful contribution to the attainment of the ideals of "freedom, justice and peace in the world" first proclaimed in 1948.

12. See various proposals in this regard in Nico Schrijver, "Fifty Years of International Covenants. Improving the Global Protection of Human Rights by Bridging the Two Covenants", in NJCM Bulletin, *Netherlands Journal of Human Rights*, Vol. 41 (2016), No. 4 (December 2016), pp. 457-464.

ICTY and the New Law on Genocide

Carsten Stahn *

A. Introduction

For a long time, there was no word for genocide. In 1915, the term crimes against humanity was used to describe the massacres of Armenians. In 1941, British Prime Minister Winston Churchill, said in a radio broadcast: "We are in the presence of the crime without a name."[1] The historical contribution of the *ad hoc* tribunals is that they made that word speakable.

With no other crime is the difference between law and semantic meaning as far divided as in relation to genocide. The word genocide has special expressive meaning. As Lemkin has shown, any attempt to reduce "genocide to law" is deemed to fail. The notion of genocide is more complex than law can describe. It is more than an attempt to describe a particular form of murder. As Hannah Arendt noted in the letters to Karl Jaspers:

> "The Nazi crimes . . . explode the limits of the law; and that is precisely what constitutes their monstrousness. For these crimes, no punishment is severe enough . . . This guilt, in contrast to all criminal guilt, oversteps and shatters any and all legal systems."[2]

Genocide has been called the crime of the 20th century. Ironically, the century nearly ended without a conviction for the crime.

---

* Professor of International Criminal Law and Global Justice at Leiden University.

1. Prime Minister Winston Churchill's broadcast to the world about the meeting with President Roosevelt on 24 August 1941.
2. Letter to Karl Jaspers, in L. Kohler and H. Saner (eds.), *Hannah Arendt/Karl Jaspers Correspondence 1926-1969* (New York, Harcourt Brace Jovanovich, 1992), pp. 51, 54.

The adoption of the Genocide Convention in 1948 by the General Assembly was not only a belated reaction to the Holocaust and the absence of genocide as a crime in the Nuremberg judgment, but as much a result of the personal efforts of Lemkin. It tried to capture the essence of genocide, yet in a significantly reduced meaning.

The Convention is special in several ways. It does not only contain an early reference to the project of international criminal jurisdiction, but included structures of state responsibility, in addition to individual criminal responsibility. It encompasses a duty of states to prevent genocide, and an express dispute settlement clause related to state responsibility for genocide.

Already in 1951, the ICJ stressed in its Advisory Opinion on *Reservations to the Convention on Genocide* case that "the origins of the Convention show that it was the intention of the United Nations to condemn and punish genocide as a crime under international law"[3]. The obligations to prevent and punish the crime of genocide was qualified as an *erga omnes* obligation.

But for a long time, the Convention was like a "new car" that did not leave the garage, to follow the famous analogy of Ian Brownlie. Lawyers, like Hersch Lauterpacht, articulated these scepticisms early on. He argued in 1955, that the Convention is more "a registration of protest against past misdeeds of individual savagery", than an "effective instrument of their prevention and repression"[4].

It is common wisdom that the definition of the Convention is strict. It requires that a national, ethnical or religious group is targeted as "such". Members must be targeted because of their belonging to a protected group. The killing of political groups was not included, since it would have opened a Pandora's box in

3. *Reservations to the Convention on the Prevention and Punishment of the Crime of Genocide* (Advisory Opinion), *ICJ Reports 1951*, 16, para. 23.
4. Lassa Oppenheim, *International Law: A Treatise*, Vol. I, 8th ed., ed. Hersch Lauterpacht (London, Longman, 1955, p. 75).

relation to internal conflicts and impeded widespread ratification at the time. The definition of the Convention implies that certain types of mass killing do not qualify as genocide.

The traditional understanding of the Convention is based on the Holocaust as a model. This is the case that drafters had in mind. Other paradigms have caused dispute. For instance it remains debated whether the Katyn massacre, which involved the killing of Polish military officers, policemen, doctors or engineers by Soviet secret police forces in 1940, qualifies as genocide. The killings were directed at members of the Polish intelligentsia. This may be a sub-group of a national group. But such sub-groups are not protected *per se*. Such incidents can only be covered by a wider interpretation which includes parts of national groups, or declares the list of protected groups as non-conclusive.

Similarly, there is controversy to what extent the acts of the Khmer Rouge regime in the late 1970s qualify as genocide. The attacks by Khmer Rouge on ethnic or religious minorities, such as Buddhist or Muslim communities, may qualify as genocide in the sense of the Convention. But the majority of victims were members within the Khmer-majority population. These members were targeted because of their belonging to specific political, professional or economic class. A UN Rapporteur coined the new term "auto-genocide" in order to distinguish this type of acts by a government against its own people from the acts through which regimes target a group which is considered as "other", such as the killing of the Jewish population and people of Slavic origin by Nazi Germany.

Much of the modern jurisprudence has been geared to adapt the genocide definition to new contexts.

In this contribution, I will first highlight how the *ad hoc* tribunals shaped a partly new approach to genocide. I will then examine some of the open challenges.

1. Emancipation from the Holocaust mode

The first international tribunal which established individual criminal responsibility for the crime of genocide was not the ICTY, but its sister tribunal the ICTR. The famous *Akayesu* case was the first genocide conviction. It is legendary in several ways.

B. The Legacy of *Akayesu*

First, in relation to its interpretation of the group requirement. The central question was whether Tutsi qualify as an ethnic group. *Akayesu* adopted an extensive interpretation of the Convention by arguing that the drafters intended to include stable and permanent groups. It defended, in particular, a subjective conception of ethnicity which takes into account societal perceptions and the socially constructed nature of ethnic identity. This interpretation reflected a sentiment in the Security Council, which had mentioned genocide in resolution 955 (1994), the founding instrument of the tribunal[5].

Second, *Akayesu* acknowledged that sexual violence, including rape can be a means of committing genocide. The Convention acknowledges that acts such as sterilization or forced procreation may amount to genocide. But few people assumed that systematic rape may be a means of committing genocide, in the sense of destroying a group. The *Akayesu* Bench found that rape and sexual violence constitute a form of serious bodily or mental harm that leads to to physical and biological destruction of Tutsi women, families and their communities[6]. *Akayesu* thus took an "intuitive and commonsensical"[7] approach to interpretation that shaped subsequent rulings.

5. SC res. 955 (1994), preamble, para. 4 ("Expressing once again its grave concern at the reports indicating that genocide and other systematic, widespread and flagrant violations of international humanitarian law have been committed in Rwanda").
6. *Akayesu*, Trial Judgment, para. 732.
7. Sluiter and Zahar, p. 172.

1. Key ICTY rulings

The ICTY developed many aspects of modern genocide law. It struggled less with the determination of ethnicity or group requirements. Its main innovation lies in the fact that it adjusted the interpretation of genocide to different contexts, in particular killings and destruction carried out against parts of groups in limited geographic areas, such as enclaves and towns. It accepted that genocide is not a game of numbers. It ruled that destruction of a part of a group is sufficient if that part is "emblematic" of the overall group.

(a) *Jelisić: Objective versus subjective interpretation*

The practice started with cases against mid- or low-level defenders. The first case, the *Jelisić* case, was a rather odd case. *Jelisić* was a 23-year-old commander at the Luka camp in Brcko who was partly deranged and presented himself as a "Serbian Adolf". He claimed to hate Muslim women and entered a guilty plea for war crimes and crimes against humanity. But he failed to acknowledge genocide.

The Trial Chamber acknowledged that genocide may exist, even when the exterminatory intent only extends to a limited geographic zone, such as a region or municipality[8]. The main problem was that Jelisić's crimes were not directly part of a broader Bosnian Serb policy to destroy the Bosnian Muslim population in Brcko. The genocide charge deviated thus clearly from the logic of the Holocaust. It was not grounded in objective factors, such as mass killings carried out according to a broader plan or policy. The

8. *Jelisić*, Trial Judgment, ICTY, 14 December 1999, para. 82.

question was whether the evil intent of a person alone can amount to genocide, even in the absence of a state or institutional policy. This issue goes to the heart of the nature of genocide, namely whether genocide should be predominantly judged by objective or naturalistic features of the crime, or by the evil intent of the perpetrator.

The first approach is more typical in relation to investigation and prosecution. Investigators or prosecutors typically look first to evidence that crimes was committed, and then analyse the relationship of the defendant to the crime. According to this logic, it must first be determined whether genocidal acts have occurred, and then it is assessed whether the person acted with genocidal intent. Such an approach may be grounded in the historic vision of genocide, its exceptional nature, and its distinction from crimes against humanity.

The second approach is more unorthodox. According to this approach, the determination of individual criminal responsibility can be supported by objective factors, such as a broader genocidal plan or policy going beyond the individual agent. But it requires primarily a consideration of the subjective intent of the accused. According to this logic, a single criminal act may amount genocide if it is carried out with intent to destroy. Technically speaking, such an understanding is not excluded by the plain wording of the convention. But it contrasts with the social understandings of genocide which tend to focus on objective events, rather than criminal intent.

In *Jelisić*, the ICTY leaned towards this second understanding. The Trial Chamber noted that "it is in fact the *mens rea* which gives genocide its speciality and distinguishes itself from an ordinary crime and other crimes against international humanitarian law"[9].

9. *Jelisić*, Trial Judgment, ICTY, 14 December 1999, para. 66.

The Chamber found that such intent could not be proven in the case at hand. But it held that the Convention does "not discount the possibility of a lone individual seeking to destroy a group as such" since "the drafters of the Convention did not deem the existence of an organisation or a system serving a genocidal objective as a legal ingredient of the crime"[10]. This point was affirmed by the Appeals Chamber, which held that the evidence at hand "could have provided the basis for a reasonable Chamber to find beyond a reasonable doubt that the respondent had the intent to destroy the Muslim group in Brcko"[11].

The *Jelisić* case had limited societal relevance. Some may argue it was trivial. But it broke important ground since it made it clear that genocide is a leadership crime. The view that genocide does not require a plan or policy became firmly embedded in jurisprudence.

Most, importantly *Jelisić* framed the methodology towards establishing genocide. As Michelle Jarvis and Alan Tieger have noted in their reflection of ICTY case law:

According to the ICTY experience, the question is not whether a particular set of crimes can be labelled in the abstract as genocide but whether the individual accused person is responsible for genocidal acts committed with genocidal intent[12].

This approach contrasts with the ICC. The Elements of Crimes contain an additional material element which requires that the

> "conduct took place in the context of a manifest pattern of similar conduct directed against that group or was conduct that could itself effect such destruction".

This threshold is specific to the ICC. It was introduced to reflect the special gravity of genocide and to avoid that isolated hate crimes fall within the ambit of ICC jurisdiction. This restriction

10. *Jelisić*, Trial Judgment, para. 100.
11. *Jelisić*, Appeal, 5 July 2001, para. 68.
12. Michelle Jarvis and Alan Tieger, "Applying the Genocide Convention at the ICTY", (2016), 14 *JICJ* 857, 869.

may be explained by the fact that the ICC has a much larger jurisdictional mandate in terms of situations than the ICTY. It was rejected by the ICTY Appeals Chamber in the *Kristić* case, which became the first genocide conviction of the ICTY[13].

(b) *Krstić*

The *Krstić* case occurred at a time when there was strong pressure on the Prosecution to bring genocide charges. It concerned Srebrenica. Srebrenica differs from systematized and massive group destruction that characterized the Holocaust. The Appeals Chamber used unusually strong words. It affirmed the need to call "the massacre at Srebrenica by its proper name: genocide"[14].

Krstić made at least two key contributions to the interpretation of genocide law.

C. Localized Genocide

The first one relates to geographical scope of genocide. *Krstić* accepted the argument that genocide may occur even when the exterminatory intent extends only to a limited geographic zone – something that has been called "localized genocide"[15]. The size of the Bosnian Muslim population in Srebrenica amounted to approximately forty thousand people prior to its capture by the VRS forces in 1995. This number constituted only a fraction of the small percentage of the overall Muslim population of Bosnia and Herzegovina at the time. *Krstić*acknowleged expressly that the importance of the Muslim community of Srebrenica "is not captured solely by its size"[16].

13. See *Kristić*, Appeals, 19 April 2004, para. 224 ("the requirement . . . Does not appear in the Genocide Convention and was not mandatd by customary international law").
14. *Kristić*, Appeal Judgment, paras. 37-38.
15. W. Schabas, "Was Genocide Committed in Bosnia and Herzegovina? First Judgments of the International Criminal Tribunal for the Former Yugoslavia", *Fordham International Law Journal* 25 (2001), 23, 42.
16. *Kristić*, Appeal Judgment, para. 15.

The Trial Chamber stated

> "physical destruction may target only a part of the geographically limited part of the larger group because the perpetrators of the genocide regard the intended destruction as sufficient to annihilate the group as a distinct entity in the geographic area at issue"[17].

This point was reaffirmed on appeal:

> "By seeking to eliminate a part of the Bosnian Muslims, the Bosnian Serb forces committed genocide. They targeted for extinction the forty thousand Bosnian Muslims living in Srebrenica, a group which was emblematic of the Bosnian Muslims in general."[18]

This interpretation is compatible with the victim-centred framing of genocide[19]. But it reduces the concept of genocide to small parts or units of a broader group. It contains at least two logical reductions. It first reduced the Bosnian Muslim population to the Bosnian Muslims in Srebrenica. It then limited the focus on a part of that sub-group, namely the destruction of militarily aged Bosnian Muslim men. As Kai Ambos has noted, the intent to destroy was thus effectively related to the destruction of a "part . . . of a part . . . of the group of Bosnian Muslims"[20].

D. Inferred Intent

Second, *Krstić* accepted that genocidal intent may be shown through circumstantial evidence. In the Holocaust, and the Rwanda, the killing of the women and children was used as an argument

17. *Kristić*, Appeal Judgment, para. 590.
18. *Kristić*, Appeal Judgment, paras. 37-38.
19. See generally C. Kress, "The ICC's First Encounter with the Crime of Genocide: The Case against Al Bashir", in Stahn, *Law and Practice* (note 43), 669; K. Ambos, "What Does "Intent to Destroy' in Genocide Mean?", *International Review of the Red Cross* 91 (2009), 833.
20. Ambos Treatise, p. 43.

to support the establishment of genocidal intent. In the context of Srebrenica, the order to kill related only to the destruction of around 7,000 military-aged men and boys in Srebrenica. The Prosecution argued that the intent to kill the men and boys was to eliminate the community as a whole. The sense of destruction went further than biological or physical destruction. It claimed that the

> "community survives in many cases only in the biological sense, nothing more. It's a community in despair; it's a community clinging to memories; it's a community that is lacking leadership; it's a community that's a shadow of what it once was."

The *Krstić* judgment used three main arguments:

> "First, Bosnian Serb forces could not have failed to know 'that this selective destruction of the group would have a lasting impact upon the entire group'. Their death 'precluded any effective attempt by the Bosnian Muslims to recapture the territory'."[21]

Second, "the Bosnian Serb forces had to be aware of the catastrophic impact that the disappearance of two or three generations of men would have on the survival of a traditionally patriarchal society"[22].

Third, "the combination of those killings with the forcible transfer of the women, children and elderly would inevitably result in the physical disappearance of the Bosnian Muslim population at Srebrenica"[23].

This inference of intent was not without critics. For instance, William Schabas argued that this reasoning "distort[ed] the definition unreasonably"[24]. He argued that the intent to have a "lasting impact

21. *Kristić*, Appeal Judgment, para. 595.
22. *Ibid.*
23. *Ibid.*
24. Schabas (note 100), at 47.

on the group" is not the same as physical destruction, and that there may have been other plausible explanations for the destruction of 7,000 men and boys in Srebrenica[25].

The *Krstić* approach is both strict and flexible at the same time. It is strict in the sense that it treats genocide formally as a special intent crime, driven by the genocidal purpose of the perpetrator. The ICTY did not adopt the so-called knowledge-based approach, according to which genocide may be shown if a perpetrator contributes to collective genocidal plan or campaign with the knowledge that these actions lead to the destruction of the group. In *Krstić*, the Appeals Chamber overturned the Trial Chamber's argument that General *Krstić* shared genocidal intent. He was not found guilty as a main perpetrator, but only as an aider or abetter to genocide, since he was aware of intent to commit genocide on the part of some members of the Bosnian Serb Army.

The approach is flexible in its treatment of means of proof. It is impossible to look into the mind of perpetrators. Genocide is a collective crime. Intent was thus inferred from objective circumstances, "such as the general context, the perpetration of other culpable acts systematically directed against the same group, the scale of atrocities committed, the systematic targeting of victims on account of their membership in a particular group, the repetition of destructive and discriminatory acts, or the existence of a plan or policy"[26].

Formally, the ICTY sought to distinguish intent from personal motives of perpetrator. But this distinction is often difficult to draw. The subjective intent to destroy is *de facto* shown with reference to objective genocidal acts. In some cases, such as *Stakić*, the ICTY denied intent in cases in which the defendant was driven by goals or motives that that go beyond the destruction of the group. In the

25. Schabas, at 46-47.
26. See *Tolimir*, Trial Judgment, para. 745.

Karadžić trial judgment, the Chamber made a double inference. It first inferred knowledge from coded conversations with Miroslav Deronji, the civilian administrator of the Srebrenica region[27]. It then derived *Karadžić*'s intent from the inferred knowledge, implying that he must have had genocidal intent[28].

Krstić marked thus to some extent a point of no return, both in moral and in legal terms. No other Chamber has called into question the qualification of Srebrenica as genocide.

In 2007, the International Court of Justice showed a great degree of deference on this point to the ICTY in the *Genocide* case. It relied heavily on *Krstić* and found that the "Court has no reason to depart from the Tribunal's determination that the necessary specific intent *(dolus specialis)* was established".

(c) *Tolimir*

In 2012, this argument was extended to Žepa – the other Bosnian Muslim "safe zone" overtaken in July 1995 by the Bosnian Serbs.

The *Tolimir* Trial Chamber held, by majority, that the removal of the Bosnian Muslim civilian population from Žepa, the demolition of their homes and the mosque, and the killing three of the most prominent local leaders, amounted to genocide.

The *Tolimir* case raised the relationship between physical or biological destruction and forced transfer. Typically, there was an emphasis on killing as an essential feature of genocide. In *Tolimir*, the Appeals Chamber addressed for the first time the commission of genocide through acts other than killings, in particular forcible transfers of civilians. The Appeals Chamber clarified that forced

27. See *Karadžić*, Trial Judgment, para. 5805.
28. *Karadžić*, Trial Judgment, para. 5830. For a discussion, see M. Sterio, "The Karadzic Genocide Conviction: Inferences, Intent and the Necessity to Redefine Genocide", *Emory International Law Review* 31 (2017), 271, 289.

displacement of a population does not constitute in and of itself a genocidal act. But it admitted that forcible transfers of civilians could, in theory, lead to conditions of life calculated to bring about the physical destruction of a protected group. Such transfers may not immediately kill the members of the group, but ultimately seek their physical destruction.

The Appeals Chamber held that "nothing in the Tribunal's jurisprudence or in the Genocide Convention provides that a forcible transfer operation may only support a finding of genocide if the displaced population is transferred to concentration camps or places of execution"[29]. It found that forcible transfer may ensure the physical destruction of the protected group by "causing serious mental harm or leading to conditions of life calculated to bring about the group's physical destruction, even if the group members are not transferred to places of execution"[30]. It argued that such transfers may "threaten the physical destruction of the group in whole or in part, because they compromise the ability of the members of the protected group to lead a normal and constructive life"[31]. It thereby equated the impossibility of leading a normal and constructive life to the threat of being destroyed.

The Appeals Chamber also recognized that expulsions are not necessarily incompatible with genocidal intent. It argued acts of forcible transfer may provide a basis for inferring the perpetrators intent to destroy, in combination with other evidence concerning the commission of large-scale killings and discriminatory actions[32]. It accepted that an expulsion may encompass a variety of destructive acts that reflect an intent to destroy a community. The reasoning recognized that genocidal intent from non-destructive acts.

29. *Tolimir*, para. 209.
30. *Ibid.*
31. *Ibid.*, para. 212.
32. *Ibid.*, para. 254.

This approach stands in a certain tension with the historical assumption that the purpose underlying the prohibition of genocide is the criminalization of conduct that seeks to destroy a protected group either physically or biologically. It was criticized by Judge Antonetti, who argued that genocidal intent can only be inferred from facts that will cause the physical or biological destruction of a group, rather that the group's expulsion.

2. The way forward

The jurisprudence of the ICTY has thus clearly given a new shape to the concept of genocide. It has operated within the confines of the Convention. The tribunal has not gone so far as to endorse Lemkin's holistic construction of genocide which included destruction of political and social institutions, culture, language, national feelings, religion, or economic existence. It has, in principle, stayed loyal to the text of the Convention. It has admitted that the destruction of historical, cultural or religious heritage does not suffice to constitute genocide. But it has adjusted the narrow text to new scenarios.

The *ad hoc* tribunals have not felt constrained by the *travaux préparatoires* or historical context. As Judge Shahabuddeen put it:

> "If there is inconsistency, the interpretation of the final text of the Convention is too clear to be set aside by the *travaux*."

The modern interpretation has shown that some of the boundaries may be less clear cut than assumed. Genocide is not only about killing, but can be committed in other ways. Individual intent must be assessed in context. Destruction is mostly a process. In reality, physical or biological destruction is often connected to attacks on cultural and religious property or symbols. The two can therefore not be as neatly distinguished as the law seems to suggest.

Core aspects of the jurisprudence have been confirmed by the two genocide rulings of the International Court of Justice. But visions on the path forward remain divided. The "new law genocide" has made the distinction to crimes against humanity more fluid. Some voices contend that there is merit in a narrow legal definition, that genocides needs to remain distinct from other types of mass killings, and that the category crimes against humanity might be more appropriate to encompass new forms of violence.

Others claim that the meaning of genocide should be adjusted to new circumstances in order to avoid a growing disconnect between legal definition and public perception. They call for revision of the definition of genocide, such as the elimination of the "as such" requirement[33] or an expanded notion which might encompass "ethnic cleansing"[34], "politicide" (i.e. mass killing of political groups), "ethnocide" (i.e. destruction of language and culture for purposes of group extermination) or "gendercide" (i.e. systematic killing of members of a specific sex). Such an approach continues to meet hesitation by states, since it would broaden state obligations, expose governments to claims of state responsibility and extend civil liability for violations.

The power of the word "genocide" is thus likely to continue to exceed its legal meaning, despite the important footsteps made in the past 25 years.

---

33. Sterio, "The Karadžić Genocide Conviction", 292, noting that such an approach "would allow for acts of reprehensible persecution of members of a subgroup within one of the protected groups to constitute genocide".
34. Micol Sirkin, "Expanding the Crime of Genocide to Include Ethnic Cleansing: A Return to Established Principles in Light of Contemporary Interpretations", (2010) 33 *Seattle University Law Review* 489.

The Peace Palace and New Challenges to Peace Diplomacy

Steven van Hoogstraten

Your royal highness, excellency's, ladies and gentlemen,

Let me start this contribution with a particular case of conflict solution. It was I think two years ago (10 October 2010) that the press mentioned that Turkey and Armenia had settled certain differences between them in Switzerland. Both states had agreed to open diplomatic relations. It was at that moment that I felt with an acute flash, this could also have happened in The Hague, City of Peace and Justice. Was there a reason for these two parties to choose for one location more than for another? I did not know, I still do not know. But I was not aware then, that a long process had preceded this historic signature. A Turkish Armenian Reconciliation Commission had been created on 9 July 2001, nine years earlier. All the groundwork had been prepared there. What follows will be inspired in part by this instance.

Ladies and gentlemen,

At the time of the creation of the Peace Palace, which was in the early years of the 20th century, many people felt that international peace would be brought about by the introduction of arbitration. "Peace through law", was the early credo of the Peace Palace. The great philanthropist Andrew Carnegie, the man who gave the financial means to build this palace, was passionate about this concept. In a speech to the students of St. Andrews in Scotland in 1905, he made a strong plea for the establishment of a League of Peace, which would be able to act swiftly if international trouble would break out. This speech was held before the Second Peace Conference of The Hague of 1907, before the first World War, and well before the real League of Nations was set up in 1920. Carnegie felt that war should be abolished by the leading nations of the world, just like slavery had been abolished in the United States.

"Peace through law" still is the dominant feature of the work of the institutions in the Peace palace. The International Court of Justice has the mandate to settle international disputes in accordance with international law – Belgium/Senegal under the Anti-Torture Convention, being the latest – and to advise the institutions of the UN on matters of legal dispute. Think about the legality of the declaration of independence by Kosovo. The key question is therefore if the Peace Palace could also develop activities which fall in a different category, which are – in other words – alternative ways to settle or dismantle international conflicts. The short answer is that this seems rather attractive, as long as it is compatible with the work of the International Court of Justice and that of the Permanent Court of Arbitration. The longer answer will show a more complete picture. I will explore this in greater detail.

Ladies and gentlemen,

The Secretary-General (SG) of the UN has produced a report recently (not yet officially published) about "strengthening the role of mediation in the peaceful settlement of disputes, conflict prevention and resolution". This report is the follow-up to a request by the General Assembly (65/283). It analyses the key trends in the field of mediation. Since 2009 – the report states – parties to disputes utilized UN supported mediation and good offices in a long list of cases. In total 36 countries or regions were involved, from Afghanistan to Yemen, and including Cyprus, Côte d'Ivoire, the Great Lakes region, Iraq, Nepal, Sri Lanka and Syria, to name a few of the list. Many of these mediation efforts sought to address conflicts or disputes of a political nature. In some cases mandates from the Security Council provided the basis for conflict prevention and resolution efforts. In others, the SG of the UN just offered his good offices. Mediation efforts have also been used to address disputes and conflicts over specific issues, such as natural resources. For example, the UN regional Centre for Preventive Diplomacy in Central Asia (UNRCCA) plays an important mediation role in promoting responsible sharing and management of the region's water supply amongst the five Central Asian states, with the help of the UN's environment programme, UNEP. UNEP itself supported natural resources negotiations in the central highlands of Afghanistan, and the Mesopotamian marshlands shared by Iran and Iraq. The Secretary-General points out that not all partnership efforts (UN and local together) have been successful. This was the case in Lybia, where the UN and the African Union did not agree on a common approach and strategy.

Often the civil society is involved as well, like with the International Crisis Group – led by former Human Rights Commissioner Louise Arbour – or the Red Cross. The International Crisis Group now has a staff of 150 persons, but they started off with only a tiny office of 2 persons. The International Crisis Group is generally recognized as the world's leading independent source of advice to governments in conflict areas. It has a loud voice in conflict prevention. Their weapons are thorough analysis, and public advocacy. Former US Secretary of State Madeleine Albright called it "a full service conflict prevention organization".

What these cases show is that the United Nations is very active in many different countries, that it works both on its own behalf or acts together with local or regional mediators. And the civil society is not sitting on its hands either. There is simply a lot of international mediation going on. So we should not think or do as if we are unearthing something totally new. We should on the contrary ask ourselves if the Netherlands and more precisely the city of The Hague might produce some added value – if we could be an effective player in this rather political field.

Ladies and Gentlemen,

In this month of September, talks have started in Oslo, between the government of Colombia and the FARC movement. This emphasizes a role for Norway, which we know well. We all remember the Oslo Accords of 1993, brokered to come to peace in the Middle East. Would the Norwegian government be able to foster a peace agreement in this longstanding internal strife? In the past the Norwegian government made a point of not showing any involvement, in order not to hamper the talks, leaving it to academics to take the heat if the secrets of the talks were blown away. But in this case, there can be no doubt about the need for a role of the government. In my view it is essential for success. One of my main points is that a mediating role of this Palace, this symbol of international peace, can only be viable if there is clear support by the Netherlands government for mediations to take place in this country.

I think it was in 2003, when the SG of the UN, Kofi Annan, was in The Hague, to inaugurate the International Criminal Court. This was done on a Tuesday, so the Monday was free. He called the parties to the conflict on Cyprus to the Peace Palace, in order to reach an agreement on his plan to end the deadlock on the island originating in the forceful Turkish occupation of the northern part of Cyprus in 1974. So everyone was there, including the famous Mr. Denktash. It was an electrifying day, with a tremendous interest from the press.

The final press information was given at 04.00 hours by Kofi Annan himself, in the Great Hall of Justice. Much to the regret of Kofi Annan, the talks had not led to a positive result, even if this was within grasp. For once, the Peace Palace had been used for our subject matter of today, the holding of international peace talks. But this had never been possible with a court case or a major arbitration going on at the same time.

It is obvious to me that the Peace Palace would be very qualified to be a involved in talks and negotiations. The ambition of the Palace is to contribute to international peace, and that does include a settlement of disputes which do not – or not yet – necessitate a legal answer. We have to recognize here that many international conflicts are of a political nature and can not be framed easily as a legal matter.

Incidentally the Permanent Court of Arbitration – oldest inhabitant of the Palace – is already mandated to assist parties to a conflict in a mediation. In the 1899 Hague Convention mediation is recommended in Article 3 in the following way "The Signatory powers recommend that one or more powers, strangers to the dispute, should on their own initiative and as far as circumstances may allow, offer their good offices or mediation to the States at variance." In fact there have been 3 conciliation commissions administered by the PCA, the latest in 1955 between Greece and Italy. This conciliation was concerned with the sinking in 1940 of a Greek merchant steamer by an Italian submarine. Strangely enough, none of the PCA members have asked for these services in the years since that time, even if – according to the PCA – some arbitrations could be avoided by a late and confidential mediation.

If international mediation is to be successful, and if The Hague would really be interested to enter this field in a meaningful way, the mediation process has to be assisted or facilitated by a professional party. The key question is: who would be asked to do that, who would be a qualified party. In my view there is good reason to involve the newly created Hague Institute for Global Justice. This institute is still in its early days, but it has the mandate to contribute to the understanding and solution of international issues in a multidisciplinary way, with a high ambition of quality. This institute could be the broker, or the reference desk for parties to a conflict. The Institute for Global Justice could make the appropriate decisions when a third party intervention should be proposed, or when a group of wise men and women would be helpful in the process. The institute should be allowed to explore certain alternative options, in order to further a solution. My view of mediation is not a passive one, but one of active engagement in the exploration of solutions.

What I am thinking of is a process which is not too free of form – ideally there should be some Hague method. If parties do chose for The Hague as a venue for their talks, they should know which forms of assistance are available, and such assistance should be of interest to them. Entering the process means that parties are looking for an equitable solution. As the President of the ICJ told me in a recent meeting, even during a court case it is the freedom of the parties to come to a negotiated solution up to the very last moment. The famous example here is the case between Australia and France about the nuclear tests in the Pacific. Once the Court had decided it had jurisdiction to consider the merits of the case, the two nations felt encouraged to settle their difference by talks, rather than by a judgment where one state would always be the loser and the other the winner.

We should realize how well-equipped The Hague already would be, for such a new role. I mentioned the new Institute for Global Justice. But there is more. The Institute for Historical Reconciliation and Justice (IHJR), originally from Salzburg is now established in The Hague. It is trying to support reconciliation through a two-sided historical approach, seeking a shared narrative of a conflict and avoiding to demonize the other party. The Hague Academic Coalition is a cooperative framework of seven institutions, including the Clingendael Institute, the Institute of Social Studies, the Leiden University and the Asser Institute, and their experts might be involved in a given case. The Ministry of Foreign Affairs is in the process of profiling the Netherlands as a centre of expertise in matters of peace and justice. I expect that the Ministry of Foreign Affairs would welcome this new avenue of action for The Hague. At the same time it would constitute an innovation, compared to the international legal procedures that we have got accustomed to.

There is another element I would like to mention in connection with a mediation platform in The Hague. So far, I referred to conflicts between states, which might be solved otherwise than through a legal settlement by a court. But there is a large area of non-public, or semi-public differences, which could be eligible for mediation as well. Imagine high profile differences between an oil company and a environmental NGO for instance. I know that the Institute for Global Justice has a project about the dispute settlement in relation to problems caused by large-scale biomass production. Or think of problems between banks and groups of consumers. Or a conflict between a country and a multinational about the use of water resources it shares with other countries. These might benefit from some form of mediation as well.

We should also note that an innovative approach was presented in this same hall, in January, when private parties in the financial world inaugurated a facility for the arbitration of differences regarding financial products (PRIME). This new institution follows the same pattern as the PCA – it has a list of experts who will be called to form a tribunal in any case which is submitted to them. Clearly, this new route is an alternative to a judicial settlement, and its key advantage is the level of expertise in its procedures, a level of expertise which one would not assume with judges.

So finally my intervention boils down to the finding that a mediation or conciliation facility could well take shape in The Hague, provided that the government of the Netherlands would give such an initiative its backing. A mediation facility which has a broad entry door, so allowing for different types of conflict in the public or semi public sphere. The infrastructure for the support of the mediation should in my view be independent from the Peace Palace. This should preclude any misunderstanding about the role of the International Court of Justice. But the worldwide appeal of this Peace Palace make it very suitable to play a part at any point in the mediation proceedings. I think The Hague is ready for that. If peace can be brokered in Camp David, it can be also done in this city of The Hague.

I thank you for your attention.

Le Palais de la Paix, la CIJ et la Fondation Carnegie (Discours en l'honneur de M. Steven van Hoogstraten)

Philippe Couvreur*

Excellences,

Madame, Monsieur,

Chers amis,

M. van Hoogstraten a exercé pendant près de treize années les lourdes tâches de Directeur général de la Fondation Carnegie. Tout au long de ces années, nous avons eu le privilège de nous côtoyer au Palais de la Paix. Nous avons bien évidemment eu aussi à travailler ensemble, en nos qualités officielles respectives, nous efforçant à tout moment que ce lieu demeure le joyau au service de l'idéal pour lequel il avait été construit. Nous avons eu, à ce titre, la responsabilité de maintenir et renforcer quotidiennement, et très concrètement, dans des circonstances parfois difficiles, les liens étroits existant depuis toujours entre la Cour et la Fondation, ces liens qui font de La Haye et du Palais de la Paix les symboles mondialement reconnus de la paix et de la justice.

Nous nous sommes attachés à honorer ainsi notre dette commune à l'égard des pionniers qui ont échafaudé, à La Haye, les premiers plans d'une véritable juridiction internationale permanente. C'est en effet dans le prolongement de la première conférence de la paix, qui s'était tenue à La Haye en 1899, qu'il fut décidé de construire en cette ville un monument qui symboliserait les idéaux de paix et de justice. Grâce aux dons d'Andrew Carnegie lui-même, et aux nombreux présents offerts par des Etats du monde entier qui ornent aujourd'hui le Palais, ce magnifique projet a pu être réalisé puis développé ; on en a célébré le centenaire il y a peu.

* Greffier de la Cour internationale de Justice, depuis février 2000. Maître de conférence invité de droit international public à l'Université de Louvain, Belgique.

Le Palais de la Paix dut certes attendre quelques années, et la fin de la Première Guerre mondiale, avant d'accueillir la Cour permanente de justice internationale, prédécesseur de la Cour internationale de Justice. Le Comité consultatif de juristes, établi par la Société des Nations aux fins d'établir le Statut de la CPJI, siégea tout d'abord au Palais, au début de l'été 1920, pour remplir cette importante mission. En ce lieu, les éminents jurisconsultes accomplirent des travaux remarquables et fondateurs, marquant le souvenir et prolongeant l'œuvre des conférences de la paix de 1899 et 1907. Ils bâtirent avec succès la juridiction permanente qui devait couronner tant d'efforts menés jusqu'alors à La Haye, mais toujours restés infructueux. Ces travaux furent aussi largement visionnaires, dans la mesure où ils fondent encore intégralement, aujourd'hui, l'organisation et le fonctionnement de la Cour internationale de Justice.

On doit bien sûr au Comité des juristes de 1920, sur la proposition de son président, le Baron Descamps, le choix de fixer à La Haye le siège de la Cour. Cette recommandation fut approuvée par les organes de la Société des Nations et inscrite dans le «marbre» du Statut lui-même; La Haye demeure aujourd'hui nommément visée dans le Statut de la CIJ, privilège dont ne jouit pas la ville de New York dans la Charte de l'Organisation des Nations Unies.

Ce choix n'était pas seulement un acte de courtoisie envers le Gouvernement néerlandais et la mairie de La Haye, qui, dès 1919 avaient proposé d'accueillir la future juridiction permanente sur leur sol. Il traduisait également le sentiment unanime que les fonctions judiciaires devaient être géographiquement séparées des fonctions politiques de la Société des Nations Unies. Il matérialisait, enfin, le lien historique entre la Cour permanente de justice internationale et les espoirs de paix et de progrès juridiques nés à La Haye vingt ans plutôt. Il était bien entendu que ce serait au Palais de la Paix, où le

Bureau de la Cour permanente d'arbitrage s'était entretemps établi, que la Cour conduirait ses travaux.

Comme le rappela solennellement le ministre des Affaires étrangères des Pays-Bas, il y a près de soixante-dix ans, par l'installation dans le Palais de la Cour permanente, puis de la Cour internationale de Justice, «cet édifice [devait] accomplir la mission que son généraux fondateur américain Andrew Carnegie avait envisagée [;] ce que Carnegie avait en vue ..., c'était d'ériger un édifice destiné au règlement juridique des litiges internationaux» (Ann. CIJ 1946-1947, p. 28).

Peu après l'entrée en vigueur du Statut de la Cour permanente, des arrangements furent trouvés entre la Société des Nations et la Fondation Carnegie, afin de faciliter l'usage du Palais de la Paix par la Cour. Témoignage des liens étroits entre nos deux institutions, l'installation de la Cour au Palais fut directement à l'origine des responsabilités plus larges conférées à la Fondation Carnegie, laquelle, créée initialement pour la construction et l'entretien du bâtiment, devint à cette occasion directement responsable de l'administration complète du Palais de la Paix.

Les arrangements entre la Société des Nations et la Fondation ont été repris, lorsque la Cour internationale de Justice a été instituée, en 1946, sous la forme d'un accord entre l'Organisation des Nations Unies et la Fondation Carnegie. Ils continuent aujourd'hui, moyennant diverses adaptations apportées au fil du temps, de régir la mise à disposition permanente des locaux du Palais à la Cour, ses Membres et son Greffe. Ils ont permis que la Cour permanente, puis la Cour internationale de Justice, donnent corps en ces lieux mêmes, par leur œuvre unique, aux vœux d'édifier une véritable justice internationale, vœux parfois qualifiés naguère d'utopiques.

A l'heure de saluer le départ en retraite de M. van Hoogstraten, je ne me dois pas seulement de rappeler son attachement constant à préserver cette tradition et son souci de faciliter l'exercice, par la Cour, de ses hautes fonctions dans des conditions conformes à son rang. Au cours de son mandat, il veilla également à ce que cette tradition puisse, autant que possible, continuer à se traduire en actes et qu'elle ne soit pas un simple vestige du passé.

Nous nous sommes ainsi attelés de concert à des chantiers de modernisation importants et durables. La négociation d'un accord complémentaire entre les Nations Unies et la Fondation Carnegie ne constitue pas la moindre de ces entreprises. Un tel accord permettra en effet d'ajuster au mieux les services et les locaux mis à la disposition de la Cour par la Fondation, en tenant compte de l'accroissement des activités de la Cour et de l'augmentation de ses effectifs au cours de la dernière décennie. Par ailleurs, comme cela a été déjà rappelé par d'autres, M. van Hoogstraten, fort de son expérience unique de reconstruction et d'agrandissement des locaux de l'Académie de droit international, a orchestré avec succès la délicate opération de modernisation de la Grande salle de justice, de manière à offrir aux Membres de la Cour et aux Etats qui comparaissent devant elle, toutes les facilités requises, au XXIe siècle, pour la tenue d'audiences publiques.

Je mesure les défis quotidiens que représente l'administration d'un endroit tel que le Palais de la Paix. Cela exige notamment de tenir compte de l'importance que revêtent, chacune à leur niveau, toutes les institutions qui y sont accueillies. Nous avons toujours souhaité utilement contribuer à l'organisation de relations harmonieuses entre tous les occupants du Palais, dans l'esprit de concorde et de respect qui sied à ce monument. Et M. le Directeur van Hoogstraten a démontré son engagement pour la réalisation d'un tel objectif. Il a fallu également parfois faire face, au Palais, à des situations inattendues et difficiles, comme par exemple récemment lors de la découverte de la contamination du bâtiment des juges par de l'amiante. M. van Hoogstraten n'a pas ménagé ses efforts pour tenter de répondre aux nombreuses interrogations et inquiétudes dont nous nous sommes faits les porte-paroles. Je veux ici le remercier de sa compréhension et je me réjouis de trouver dans son successeur, M. de Baedts, une personne pleinement ouverte au dialogue et attachée à reprendre le flambeau de cette indispensable coopération.

J'ai eu le privilège d'apprendre à mieux connaître et apprécier la personnalité de M. van Hoogstraten lorsque nous nous sommes, avec d'autres amis, lancés ensemble dans la fascinante aventure du concert de l'orchestre pour la paix organisé au Palais en décembre 2014. Cet Orchestre, fondé par S. E. Miguel Angel Estrella et dirigé par Nader Abbasi, réunit trente-cinq musiciens représentant une diversité de religions, cultures et nationalités. Cet ensemble a exécuté, avec une rare maîtrise, en ces lieux symboliques, des œuvres de Mozart, Bach ou encore Mendelssohn, démontrant, une fois de plus, et de façon magistrale, que tous les hommes de bonne volonté peuvent œuvrer en parfaite harmonie et avec succès au règne de la paix.

J'ai enfin pu compter, en la personne de M. van Hoogstraten, sur un interlocuteur conscient de l'importance du bilinguisme. Cette richesse, que toutes les institutions siégeant au Palais de la Paix ont en partage, est la condition minimale du respect de la diversité culturelle. Sans cette diversité, nous manquerions aux nobles idéaux de paix et de justice universels que symbolise le Palais.

M. van Hoogstraten goûtera certainement une retraite aussi active que pleinement méritée. Nous aurons le plus grand plaisir à le retrouver fréquemment dans cette enceinte, pour laquelle il a déployé tant d'énergie. Je ne doute pas qu'il ne s'en éloignera jamais vraiment, et qu'il nous fera fréquemment l'agréable surprise de venir nous revoir.

Je vous remercie.

The Right to Food, a Standard for Civilization?*

Steven van Hoogstraten

As the General Director of the Carnegie Foundation, owner and management authority of the Peace Palace, I warmly welcome you to this Palace, in the eyes of many not only an international courthouse but also a Temple of Peace. Those were the words of Andrew Carnegie, self-declared philanthropist, who was a great believer in peace through arbitration. I have been asked to speak at this occasion in view of my varied background, which includes work for several government departments including health. I have a legal background by training, but I am not a specialist in the field of human rights, which will explain certain questions I would like to put forward.

Generally speaking , a view from the Peace Palace should always start with the emphasis on the respect for the Rule of Law. As I see it, the respect for the Rule of Law by a country means that a legal system is in place with an independent judiciary (which is not twisted by politics), and that both the public guarantees of legal protection and the accountability of leading politicians and military officials before the instances of justice are well developed. The essence is that the exercise of power is restricted by law, according to the maxim "le droit prime la force", and that the rights of the individuals can be validated and ascertained in a court of law. It is unfortunate that this is not the case in so many countries. Also countries which have included the UN conventions on Human Rights in their law books.

I have to state up front that corruption at all levels is often an important factor. Corruption is a phenomenon so widespread in

*This is the text of an address held by the author at a conference on Human Rights in the Peace Palace in January 2015.

the world, that it seems that only those nations with strong and free media can escape that form of contamination. Media will expose the wrongdoings, and call for action. If corrupt leadership cannot be held accountable before the instances of justice, where do you end and how do the human rights fit in that picture. In the debate about corruption, human rights only hold a superficial position, I am tempted to say. The UN Convention against Corruption (adopted by GA resolution 58/4 in 2003) has come into effect and now has no less than 184 state parties, but this convention is not a typical human rights instrument. In his introduction to the text of the Convention, SG Kofi Annan only mentioned human rights in passing: "Corruption is an insidious plague that has a wide range of corrosive effects on societies. It undermines democracy and the rule of law, leads to violations of human rights, distorts markets, erodes the quality of life and allows organized crime, terrorism and other threats to human security to flourish." The corruption of the political class, the industry and even – sometimes – the judiciary constitutes a world problem that we can read about every day in the international newspapers. Transparency and legal accountability procedures are important in the fight against corruption.

If we see that the latest World Report 2015 of Human Rights Watch announces human rights violations in 90 countries, we may safely assume that much of the human rights corpus is still ink on paper, rather than reality. The executive director of Human Rights Watch Kenneth Roth declared "human rights violations played a major role in spawning or aggravating many of today's crises". Protecting human rights and ensuring democratic accountability are the key to resolving them. The director of Human Rights Watch denounced the policy of countries that see the issue of human rights as a luxury, which can only be addressed in good times. Still, one may observe that most of the countries where the human rights are duly respected are countries of a democratic nature, with proper legal controls, with an open eye for the Rule of Law and for the freedom of the press.

I have asked myself, if we talk about human rights, which human rights are at stake? When the European Union drafted a set of fundamental rights, which it made a part of the treaty – first in 2000 and later in 2007 – it included not only the classical rights like freedom of expression or freedom of thought but also the right to education, to health, the right to food and to a decent environment. My remark here is, are these last issues not more a matter of government policy, than a form of human rights ? Where exactly is the dividing line between the fundamental rights of any individual and the obligation of a state to work in the interest of its citizens. Or is it all the same story, basically another way to formulate policies beneficial to the people ?

Let me take the *right to food* as an example. The *right to food* is seen as a human right protecting the right for people to feed themselves in dignity. This will imply that sufficient food is available, that people have the means to access it, and that it adequately meets the individuals' dietary needs. The right to food – we can reason – protects the right of all human beings to be free from hunger and malnutrition, free from food insecurity, and free from the scandalous and immoral starvation policies of some countries in times of conflict. So it is a wide-ranging, and very important concept. But *the right to food* does not imply that governments have an obligation to hand out free food to everyone who wants it, or a right for the individual to be fed. This particular right to food is derived from the International Covenant on Economic, Social and Cultural Rights (1966), with 160 state parties and later reaffirmed by the World Food Summit. The right to food is a typically positive right, in the sense that governments have to act to make it a reality. But it is also a normal government task, which should flow from any decent administration: a public task of every nation not to leave its population starve or accept it to be undernourished. There is, as far as I know of, no way to claim this right to food anywhere. It is therefore a very neat and political expression, but not a right in the traditional sense. The EU did not include the right to food in its Charter on Fundamental Rights, which sort of proves the point. The EU was slightly concerned about the consequences of adopting a "right to food".

The EU stated that the Charter of Fundamental Rights is aimed at a "peaceful future based on common values" (Preamble) and that it "confirms the rights as they result from the constitutional traditions and the international obligations common to the Members States" *(ibid.)*. This is an interesting formula as it refers to the constitutional traditions of the Member States as the co-origin of the rights of the individual. The EU has – however – been careful not to use a language that would create rights for citizens *per se*. The Charter is addressed to the institutions of the EU, and to the Member States when they apply European law. The Member States of the EU have tried, but probably in vain, to limit the impact of this Charter to the subject matters and areas within their control[1].

The whole concept of human rights has had a tremendous impact on international relations. My own country, the Netherlands, has made the respect for human rights a central element of its foreign policy, supported by a special ambassador for human rights. If a serious breach of human rights is reported, the Netherlands government will have to wave the finger and speak to the government in question and express its concerns and discontent. This happens before all other matters, like trade or the economy or bilateral issues. Such is the instruction of the parliament, and the media are very sensitive and keen to the follow-up. If you are in favour of an absolute protection of human rights you are

1. Charter of Fundamental Rights of the European Union, Official Journal, 2007/C 303/1.

considered a progressive, if you take a more cautious line you are seen as a conservative who is easily painted as co-responsible for atrocious facts. Unnecessary to say, that the constant climbing of the moral high ground by the defenders of human rights may have some negative effects in international relations as well.

In general international theory, the law of nations is formed by states. Obligations and rights are formulated for states, so can the rights of an individual be part of that international legal system? There is no doubt that the global human rights conventions are part of the general body of international law. If one sees the level of violation of human rights, it is quite baffling to note that the human rights treaties are formally subscribed to by no less than 168 nations of the world, from Afghanistan to Zimbabwe. China signed but did not ratify the UN Treaty on Civil and Political Rights.

My point so far is that the notion of human rights is more of a political and social desirability than a hard and fast rule under international law. More like a code of behaviour, than a practically enforceable obligation. Therefore, it is my perception that governments would be well advised not to enlarge the notion of human rights too much, and not try to define each international issue as a human rights violation. Better to try to stick to the traditional liberties of mankind, the protection of the traditional liberties of the individual. We should furthermore realize that these liberties are very much an invention of the modern western world, and that there are other parts of the world where the wellbeing of the collectivity is placed at a higher ranking than the rights of the individual. I remember a leading religious representative from the Arab world express this in public during a high-level interreligious debate in the Peace Palace. In his eyes the interests of the individual person have a lower priority than the interests of the collectivity of people. Human rights have to be seen as rights of the population at large, not as the rights of the individual. This man came from a country where women do not yet have the right to vote.

To stay on the positive side, let us note that on a regional level in some parts of the world, the protection of the fundamental rights of man is well developed, or at least developed to a certain degree. I refer to the European Convention and the European Court of Human Rights in Strasbourg, the Inter American Court of Human Rights in San José, Costa Rica, and the African Court on Human and Peoples' Rights in Arusha, Tanzania. In the first, the European case, an individual can bring a case against a state, but in the African example, this is only possible if the state concerned has allowed for this option (only 5 states have done so). Otherwise it is a matter of state versus state, like the situation is before the ICJ. The ICJ is not considered to be a "human rights court" *per se*, but it has made important contributions to this field of law. I am sure that their practice will be alluded to in greater detail by others, but is worth noting that where a system exists of verification and judgment, the protection of human rights has a set of teeth which otherwise is lacking. I should of course add the tremendous work of the UN Human Rights Council in Geneva. Personally I think that the monitoring by this council comes close to creating a world conscience on human rights, just by the naming and shaming of those countries and governments that have failed to live up to the human rights standard.

I think that we should spend some time on the question why it is that so many governments have introduced limitations on the freedom of expression. The leadership did not want to be criticized, did not want to be weakened by the exposure to liberal thinkers and critics who could easily influence the general mood in the country. I remember my visit as a health official to Cuba, where I wanted to go to a book shop. But there was no book shop in the whole of Havana, and the scarcely available newspaper stands were filled with only the copies of a 4-page government newspaper called the "Grandma". That was the name of the ship that carried the revolutionaries to the shores.

The opposition between the international law concerned with the rights of individuals and the law related to state sovereignty was very present at a colloquium organized by the ICJ on the occasion of the centenary of the Peace Palace in 2013. It became clear to me that theories on the matter diverge, and that strong arguments can be developed on both sides of the house. A new law for humankind versus states as the sole subjects and architects of international law. We may be on the way to a situation where the rights of individuals are part of the international legal order, but in my view we are still far from having accepted the relative reduction of the position of states as the sole architects of international law.

I would like to return to the question where the human rights are specific for the individual, and where the so-called rights are more the expression of a desired policy. If one says that the individual has a right to live in a drugs-free environment, or that he or she has a right to health or to proper education, I see these elements more as a moral instruction to the government concerned. As I know from experience of 25 years as a government agent, there are always many competing claims on a specific issue, the budget not being the last of those. And within an administration there are always diverging views. So to claim an absolute right for the individual is in my eyes simply a bridge too far, even if the moral instruction of the standard in question ("everyone is entitled to a right to food") can play political role in the debate.

The concept of the role of human rights in the international legal order is a popular theme for The Hague Academy of International Law, which holds annual courses in the summer for some 600 students from all parts of the world. I have tried to count the academic courses devoted to this issue, but the number of hits was too great. Let me just state that this year's Study Centre, which brings young researchers to The Hague for 3 weeks, will be devoted to the subject of "the access of the individual to international justice". I hope that the young researchers will show us how far the glass of individual rights has been filled in the past decades, and whether we may now see this as a standard for civilization.

Closing Statement

Steven van Hoogstraten

Your exellencies, ladies and gentlemen,

I would like to thank you all for having participated in this seminar, and in particular the speakers for their interesting contributions. It is gratifying to see that what started as a basic question about the actual place of the Peace Palace in the international scene of dispute settlement, came to fruition in this way. What does that world of conflict resolution look like at present? Which approaches are most appropriate to be effective, and is our iconic Peace Palace – as one says – "ready for the future". It has become clear to me that state to state disputes still play a dominant role, but also that the menu offers substantially more than that. I hope that what was said here will have some staying power in the debates that follow.

For me this was the last chapter in my work for the Carnegie Foundation and The Hague Academy of International Law. It has been a prestigious, rewarding and often challenging position to hold. Different institutions need to organize their life here in the Peace Palace, and programmes or ambitions could overlap. That is where the Foundation had to prove its worth and fortunately most of the times a positive accommodation was found. But sometimes there were no simple solutions. To my friends and colleagues in the Peace Palace I would like to point to the expression that nothing shines if you do not rub it first.

I am deeply happy that the issue of asbestos is largely – or should I still say: in part – behind us, now that the renovation of the Judges Wing has been completed. I understand that judges and staff will return to their regular premises in a matter of days. Yesterday I saw the present state of the Judges Wing – it definitely has been given a modern and quality look and feel. I know that my successor Eric de Baedts still has a lot on his plate. I will not dwell on that but I wish him all the best from here.

I would like to thank my Board, and in particular chairman Bernard Bot, for all the support and guidance. He has been involved in many of the developments over the past period, like – *inter alia* – the start of the Visitor Centre and final stages of the renovation of this Great Hall of Justice – apart from his work for The Hague Academy

To work for the Peace Palace is both a privilege and a bit of an adventure. A task of many facets like being host to the institutions, overseeing building projects, promoting academic publishing, finding of restoration funds, finding of funds for The Hague Academy, managing events, enhancing the public face of the Palace, and so on. When we had to shape up the centenary celebrations of the Palace in 2013, we realized that this could not be just a local event. A solid cooperation with the City of The Hague and the Ministry of Foreign Affairs created the basis. Your indulgence with the programme we came up with, including a full-blown peace concert in the garden of the Palace, was much appreciated. You have all made a great contribution to the unique event, and together is was really something special. United Nations Secretary-General Ban Ki-moon declared at the official commemoration day that The Hague is indeed the legal capital of the world, the epicentre of justice and accountability.

I do thank Registrar Philippe Couvreur for his very kind words. We have faced the day-to-day problems in the Peace Palace, both in French and in English. We needed to preserve the dignity of this place while opening up to tourists and events. The Peace Palace has a strong, a very strong appeal to the outside world, and the Foundation tries to be receptive to that appeal where this is compatible with the activities of the ICJ and the PCA. Our joint effort to bring the Arab/Israeli "Orchestre pour la paix" to The

Hague was rewarded with success, not least because this venture was supported by so many ambassadors and institutions. A great event it was, with high symbolic value. Both in this Palace and in the Kloosterkerk.

Before I hand back to chairman Bot, allow me one last comparison. This comparison comes from the lyrics of the famous song *Hotel California* by the group the Eagles, a classic world hit that ends up top of the charts all the time. In the last line of the song the night watchman of the hotel says to the guest who tries – in vain – to find the exit door, he says "Relax, we are programmed to receive, you can check out any time you like, but you can never leave."

I know the exit of the Peace Palace full well, but the sentence from this song sums up nicely how I felt and feel about the Peace Palace.

I thank you for your kind attention.

www.ingramcontent.com/pod-product-compliance
Lightning Source LLC
Chambersburg PA
CBHW031326230926
51848CB00001B/108
* 9 7 8 9 0 0 4 3 8 4 2 8 6 *